50 Days
of Korean 1

50일 완성 한국어 1
50 Days of Korean 1

초판 1쇄 발행 2025년 4월 30일

지은이 김은아·장은아

펴낸곳 서울대학교출판문화원
주소 08826 서울 관악구 관악로 1
도서주문 02-889-4424, 02-880-7995
홈페이지 www.snupress.com
페이스북 @snupress1947
인스타그램 @snupress
이메일 snubook@snu.ac.kr
출판등록 제15-3호

ISBN 978-89-521-3219-2 04710
    978-89-521-3957-3 (세트)

ⓒ 김은아·장은아, 2025

이 책은 저작권법에 의해서 보호를 받는 저작물이므로
무단 전재와 복제를 금합니다.

50 Days of Korean 1

김은아·장은아 지음

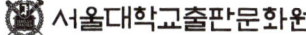

머리말

한국과 한국 문화에 대한 관심으로 한국어를 배우고자 하는 학습자들이 많이 늘어나고 있습니다. 『50일 완성 한국어 1』은 한국어 학습에 많은 시간을 할애하기 어려운 학습자들이 쉽고 가볍게 한국어를 배우고 익힐 수 있도록 구성한 자율학습용 교재입니다.

『50일 완성 한국어 1』은 한국어를 처음 접하는 학습자들이 친숙한 일상적인 주제와 기능에 대한 언어 사용 능력을 익혀 기초적인 한국어 의사소통 능력을 기르는 것을 목표로 합니다.

한 과는 네 페이지로 구성되어 있어서 부담 없이 매일 학습이 가능하며 배운 내용을 실제 생활에 바로 적용할 수 있게 함으로써 학습 효능감을 높일 수 있도록 구성했습니다.

'듣기→말하기→읽기→쓰기'의 단계적 구성을 통해 책의 흐름을 따라가다 보면 자연스럽게 학습 목표에 다다를 수 있도록 구성했습니다.

매 과마다 대화 상황을 그림으로 제시하여 대화 상황/맥락을 파악하도록 구성했습니다. 또한 목표 대화를 음성으로 제시하고 그것을 따라해 봄으로써 '듣고 말하기' 활동이 가능하도록 구성했습니다. 그와 함께 대화 내용 중 학습 목표가 되는 부분을 밑줄로 제시해 직접 써보도록 함으로써 '읽고 쓰기' 활동이 가능하도록 구성하였으며 이러한 활동을 통해 언어의 네 가지 기능이 통합되고 고루 향상될 수 있도록 했습니다.

각 과마다 간단한 퀴즈를 제시하여 배운 내용을 부담 없이 확인하고 활용할 수 있도록 구성했습니다.

핵심적인 문법 항목과 필수 어휘, 그리고 해당 과의 의사소통 목표 달성에 필요한 핵심 표현들에 대한 설명을 번역과 함께 제시함으로써 쉽고 유의미한 학습이 이루어질 수 있도록 구성했습니다.

각 과마다 주제와 관련된 흥미로운 한국 문화를 사진과 함께 제시하였습니다. 한국어를 더욱 잘하고 한국을 더 많이 이해하기 위해서 꼭 알아야 할 한국어의 특징과 다양한 한국 문화를 제시함으로써 한국에 대한 이해를 높이고 보다 흥미롭게 학습에 참여할 수 있도록 구성했습니다.

단지 50일 동안의 학습을 통해 한국어 표준교육과정의 1단계에 해당하는 기초적인 한국어 의사소통 수준에 이를 수 있도록 여러분을 안내하는 『50일 완성 한국어 1』은 여러분의 한국어 학습에 자신감과 만족감을 드릴 것입니다.

Introduction

Interest in Korea and its culture is inspiring more people to learn Korean. *50 Days of Korean (1)* is a self-study textbook designed for busy learners who want to study Korean in an easy and accessible way.

This book aims to help first-time learners develop basic communication skills by introducing familiar topics and practical grammar used in daily life. Each four-page unit is designed to be completed easily in a single day. The content is structured for immediate use in daily life, enhancing learning effectiveness.

Following the book's step-by-step approach in listening, speaking, reading, and writing will help you naturally reach your learning goals. Each unit includes illustrated dialogues to help you understand the situation and context more easily. Recordings of the target dialogues support listening and speaking practice, while fill-in-the-blank exercises reinforce reading and writing skills. These activities integrate all four language skills for balanced development. Simple quizzes in each unit allow you to review and apply what you have learned.

Key grammar points, vocabulary, and expressions are translated to facilitate learning and enhance understanding. Each unit also introduces an interesting aspect of Korean culture or language, illustrated with photographs and connected to the unit's theme. These cultural sections will enhance your understanding of Korea and inspire you to learn more.

50 Days of Korean (1) guides you to achieving basic communication skills in Korean, aligned with level one of the standard Korean curriculum, in just 50 days. We hope this book will give you confidence and satisfaction in learning Korean.

교재 구성 Unit Organization

그림을 보면서 어떤 내용인지 추측하며 목표 대화를 들어 보는 단계입니다. 들은 내용의 의미를 확인할 수 있도록 한국어와 함께 번역이 제시됩니다.

In this step, listen to the target dialogue while looking at the picture and guessing what it's about. A translation is provided alongside the Korean so that you can check the meaning of what you heard.

앞에서 들은 내용을 따라해 보는 단계입니다. 또한 말풍선으로 제시된 대화의 내용을 읽고 밑줄 친 부분을 써 봄으로써 자신이 듣고 말해 본 내용을 문자로 확인해 볼 수 있습니다.

Next, listen to the dialogue and repeat what you heard. You can also read the provided dialogue and fill in the blanks to check the written form of what you've already heard and spoken.

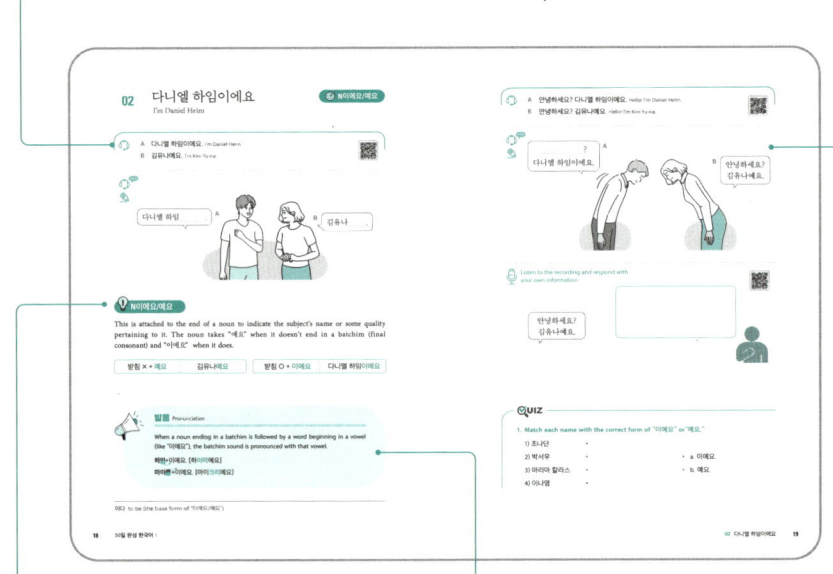

초급 단계에서 꼭 알아야 하는 문형에 대한 핵심적이고 간결한 설명이 일상생활에서 자주 쓰이는 예문과 함께 제시되어 학습자가 정확하고 자연스러운 한국어를 학습할 수 있도록 합니다.

A simple, bare-bones explanation of grammar constructions that are essential in the early stage of learning Korean is provided along with example sentences that are often used in everyday life. These explanations help you learn Korean that's both natural and accurate.

해당 과의 어휘나 문형과 관련된 발음 규칙과 억양 등을 제시하여 말하기의 정확성과 유창성을 기르도록 합니다.

Intonation and pronunciation rules that are related to the unit's vocabulary and grammar are provided to develop the accuracy and fluency of your speaking skill.

학습자의 흥미와 관심을 유발하는 현대 한국의 생활, 제도, 언어 표현 등의 문화 항목이 설명되어 학습자의 한국 문화에 대한 이해를 높입니다.
Fascinating aspects of Korean culture, including contemporary lifestyle, practices, and linguistic expressions, are explained to aid your understanding of Korean culture.

해당 과의 의사소통 목표 달성에 필요한 추가적인 핵심 표현들을 문법적으로 분석하지 않고 덩어리 표현으로 제시하여 자연스럽고 원활한 한국어 구사가 가능하도록 합니다.
Other key expressions that are needed to achieve the communicative goals of each unit are provided as chunks without grammatical analysis to facilitate your smooth and natural command of Korean.

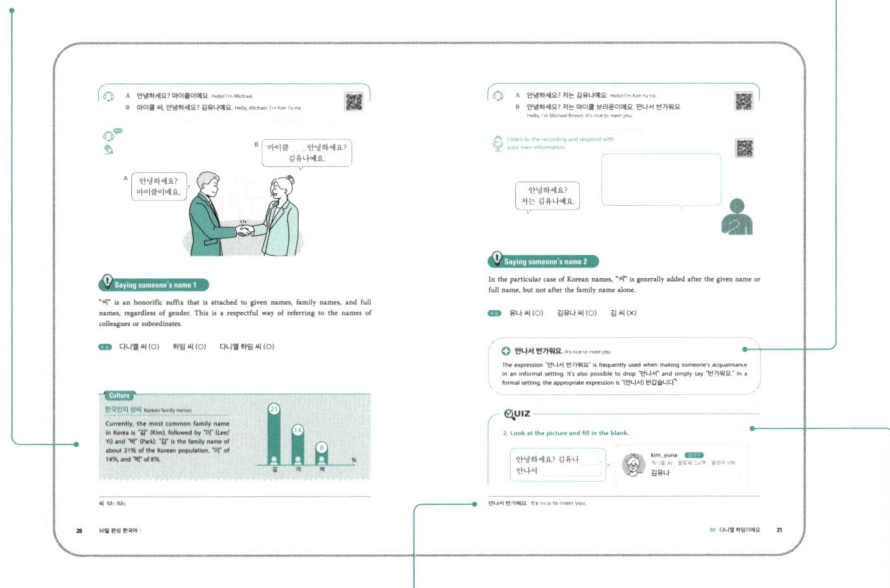

새 단어가 교재 하단에 번역과 함께 제시되어 학습자들의 어휘 학습을 돕습니다.
New words are listed at the bottom of each page along with a translation to assist your vocabulary acquisition.

학습한 내용과 관련된 간단한 퀴즈는 학습자가 배운 내용을 바로 확인하고 성취감을 느낄 수 있도록 돕습니다.
Simple quizzes about the learning material help you immediately review what you've learned and feel a sense of accomplishment.

차례 Contents

머리말 Introduction　　4
교재 구성 Unit Organization　　8

01 안녕하세요?　14
Hello!

02 다니엘 하임이에요　18
I'm Daniel Heim

03 저는 독일 사람이에요　22
I'm German

04 저는 학생이 아니에요　26
I'm Not a Student

05 지금 공부해요　30
I'm Studying Right Now

06 커피를 좋아해요　34
I Like Coffee

07 고기를 안 먹어요　38
I Don't Eat Meat

08 집에 가요　42
I'm Going Home

09 집에서 밥을 먹어요　46
I Eat Meals at Home

10 오늘 수업이 없어요　50
I Don't Have Class Today

11 물냉면 주세요　54
I Would Like Some Mul-Naengmyeon

12 참치김밥 하나 주세요　58
I Would Like One Tuna Gimbap

13 맥주 두 병하고 소주 한 병 주세요　62
Two Bottles of Beer and One Bottle of Soju, Please

14 천 원이에요　66
It's 1,000 Won

15 양념치킨이 맛있어요　70
Yangnyeom Chicken Tastes Good

16 저녁에 운동을 해요　74
I Exercise in the Evening

17 몇 시에 일어나요?　78
What Time Do You Get Up?

18 네 시부터 일곱 시까지 아르바이트를 해요　82
My Part-Time Work Goes from Four to Seven O'Clock

19 무슨 요일에 아르바이트를 해요?　86
What Days of the Week Do You Work Part-Time?

20	생일이 언제예요? 90 When Is Your Birthday?	30	그냥 집에서 쉬려고 해요 130 I'm Just Planning to Relax at Home
21	전화번호가 어떻게 돼요? 94 Can You Tell Me Your Phone Number?	31	기차로 부산에 갈 거예요 134 I'm Going to Go to Busan by Train
22	은행이 어디에 있어요? 98 Where Is the Bank?	32	부산까지 얼마나 걸려요? 138 How Long Does It Take to Get to Busan?
23	아래층으로 가세요 102 Go Downstairs	33	집에 걸어서 가요 142 I Go Home on Foot
24	어제 집에서 쉬었어요 106 I Rested at Home Yesterday	34	KTX가 아주 빨라요 146 The KTX Is Very Fast
25	책을 읽고 잤어요 110 I Read a Book and Went to Bed	35	머리가 아파요 150 My Head Hurts
26	순두부찌개가 맵지만 맛있어요. 114 Sundubu-jjigae Is Spicy, but It Tastes Good	36	오늘 날씨가 추워요 154 The Weather Is Cold Today
27	유튜브를 보거나 책을 읽어요 118 I Watch YouTube or Read a Book	37	어느 계절을 좋아해요? 158 Which Season Do You Like?
28	빨래나 청소를 해요 122 I Do the Laundry or the Cleaning	38	추워서 겨울을 안 좋아해요 162 I Don't Like Winter Because It's Cold
29	방학에 고향에 갈 거예요 126 I'm Going to Go to My Hometown for the Vacation	39	눈이 많이 와서 산에 못 갔어요 166 It Snowed a Lot, So I Couldn't Go to the Mountain

㊵	누구의 가방이에요? 170 Whose Bag Is It?	㊼	집에 가서 밥을 먹어요 198 I'm Going Home to Eat
㊶	동생한테 선물을 보내려고 해요 174 I'm Planning to Send a Present to My Younger Sibling	㊽	다시 한번 말해 주세요 202 Please Say That One More Time
㊷	친구한테서 꽃을 받았어요 178 I Got Flowers from a Friend	㊾	오늘은 좀 쉬고 싶어요 206 I Want to Rest a Little Today
㊸	옷을 사러 백화점에 갈 거예요 182 I'm Going to Go to the Department Store to Buy Clothes	㊿	시험이 있어서 공부해야 돼요 210 There's a Test, So I Have to Study
㊹	같이 저녁을 먹을래요? 186 Would You Like to Have Dinner with Me?		
㊺	몇 시에 만날까요? 190 What Time Should We Meet?	부록	정답 Answer Key 216 어휘 색인 Vocabulary Index 223
㊻	토요일에 같이 저녁을 먹어요 194 Let's Have Dinner Together on Saturday		

50 Days
of Korean

01 안녕하세요?
Hello!

A 안녕하세요? Hello!
B 안녕하세요? Hello!

💡 Expressions used to say hello 1

"안녕하세요?" is the typical expression used when greeting someone. It's generally accompanied by a courteous nod of the head. This greeting can be used at any time of day: morning, afternoon, or evening.

➕ **안녕하십니까?** Hello! (formal speech style)
"안녕하십니까?" is the greeting used in a more official or formal situation.

안녕하세요? Hello (informal polite speech style)   안녕하십니까? Hello (formal polite speech style)

A 안녕? Hi!
B 안녕? Hi!

Expressions used to say hello 2

"안녕?" is a greeting used by younger people who have a close relationship. Koreans often accompany this greeting with a casual wave, but they do not nod their head in this case.

 안녕 Hi! (casual speech style)

"안녕" is used not only when people see each other but also when they part ways. In that case, the phrase functionally means "goodbye."

Culture

한국의 인사 A unique Korean greeting

"안녕하세요?" is the typical way that Koreans say hello, but there are other ways to greet people, too. When Koreans run into someone they know, they often ask, "밥 먹었어요?" (Have you eaten?) This greeting is comparable to the English phrase "How are you?" and is usually not intended literally. So if a Korean asks you, "밥 먹었어요?" you don't need to say what you ate or explain why you haven't eaten yet. Just say "네, 먹었어요" (Yes, I have).

QUIZ

1. Draw a line between the matching phrases.

1) 안녕? •   • a. Hello! (polite speech style)

2) 안녕하세요? •   • b. Hi! (casual speech style)

안녕 Hi (casual speech style)

A 안녕히 가세요. Goodbye.
　　B 안녕히 계세요. Goodbye.

💡 Expressions used to say goodbye 1

- "안녕히 가세요" (which literally means "go in peace") is said to the person who is leaving.
- "안녕히 계세요" (which literally means "stay in peace") is said to the person who is staying.

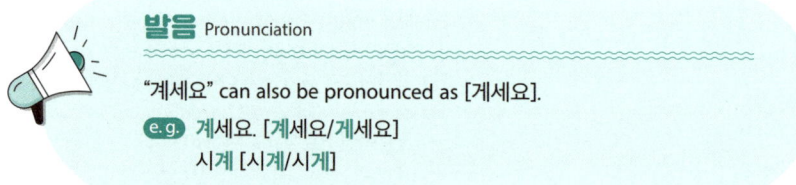

발음 Pronunciation

"계세요" can also be pronounced as [게세요].

e.g. 계세요. [계세요/게세요]
　　시계 [시계/시게]

안녕히 가세요 Goodbye (go in peace)　　안녕히 계세요 Goodbye (stay in peace)

A 안녕히 계세요. Goodbye.
B 안녕히 계세요. Goodbye.

A 안녕히 _____.

B 안녕히 _____.

💡 Expressions used to say goodbye 2

When ending a phone call, both parties use the expression "안녕히 계세요."

🔍 QUIZ

2. Draw a line between the matching phrases.

1) 안녕히 가세요. •   • a. Goodbye. (go in peace)

2) 안녕히 계세요. •   • b. Goodbye. (stay in peace)

3. Check the correct answer.

Q: 안녕하세요?
A: ☐ 안녕히 계세요.
   ☐ 안녕하세요?
   ☐ 안녕히 가세요.

다니엘 하임이에요
I'm Daniel Heim

A 다니엘 하임이에요. I'm Daniel Heim.
B 김유나예요. I'm Kim Yu-na.

다니엘 하임_____.   김유나_____.

N이에요/예요

This is attached to the end of a noun to indicate the subject's name or some quality pertaining to it. The noun takes "예요" when it doesn't end in a batchim (final consonant) and "이에요" when it does.

| 받침 ✕ + 예요 | 김유나예요 | | 받침 ○ + 이에요 | 다니엘 하임이에요 |

발음 Pronunciation

When a noun ending in a batchim is followed by a word beginning in a vowel (like "이에요"), the batchim sound is pronounced with that vowel.

하임+이에요. [하이미에요]
마이클+이에요. [마이크리에요]

이다 to be (the base form of "이에요/예요")

A 안녕하세요? 다니엘 하임이에요. Hello! I'm Daniel Heim.
B 안녕하세요? 김유나예요. Hello! I'm Kim Yu-na.

Listen to the recording and respond with your own information.

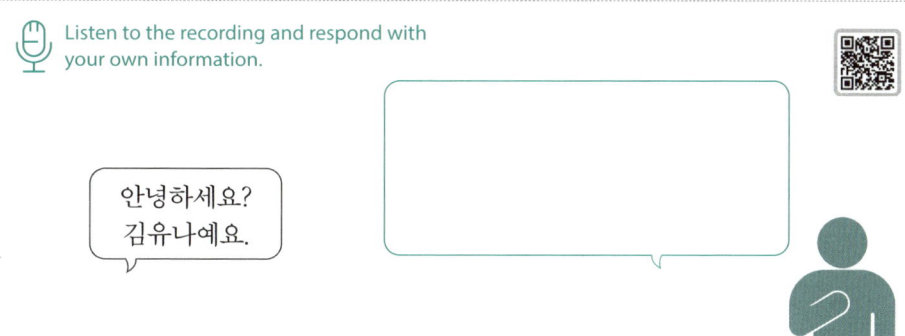

✓UIZ

1. Match each name with the correct form of "이에요" or "예요."

1) 조나단 •
2) 박서우 • • a. 이에요.
3) 마리아 칼라스 • • b. 예요.
4) 이나영 •

A 안녕하세요? 마이클이에요. Hello! I'm Michael.
B 마이클 씨, 안녕하세요? 김유나예요. Hello, Michael. I'm Kim Yu-na.

💡 Saying someone's name 1

"씨" is an honorific suffix that is attached to given names, family names, and full names, regardless of gender. This is a respectful way of referring to the names of colleagues or subordinates.

 다니엘 씨 (○)   하임 씨 (○)   다니엘 하임 씨 (○)

Culture

한국인의 성씨 Korean family names

Currently, the most common family name in Korea is "김" (Kim), followed by "이" (Lee/Yi) and "박" (Park). "김" is the family name of about 21% of the Korean population, "이" of 14%, and "박" of 8%.

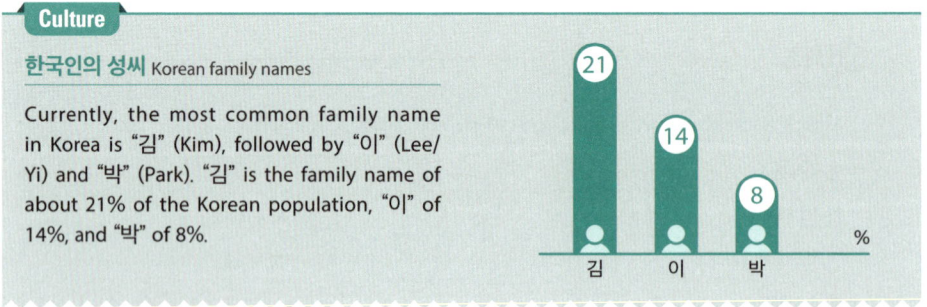

씨　Mr./Ms.

A 안녕하세요? 저는 김유나예요. Hello! I'm Kim Yu-na.
B 안녕하세요? 저는 마이클 브라운이에요. 만나서 반가워요.
Hello, I'm Michael Brown. It's nice to meet you.

Listen to the recording and respond with your own information.

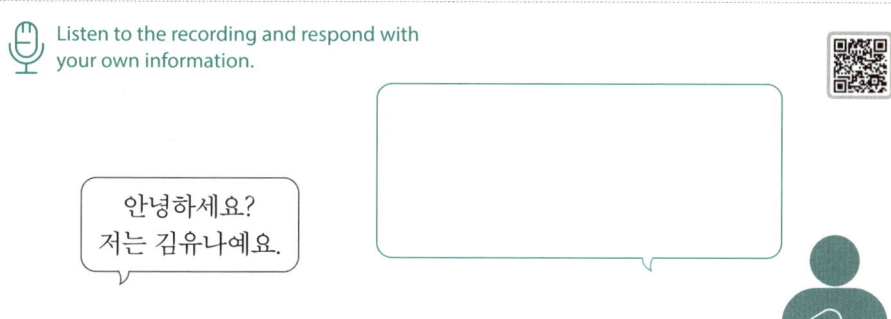

안녕하세요? 저는 김유나예요.

Saying someone's name 2

In the particular case of Korean names, "씨" is generally added after the given name or full name, but not after the family name alone.

 유나 씨 (○)   김유나 씨 (○)   김 씨 (✗)

> ➕ **만나서 반가워요.** It's nice to meet you
>
> The expression "만나서 반가워요" is frequently used when making someone's acquaintance in an informal setting. It's also possible to drop "만나서" and simply say "반가워요." In a formal setting, the appropriate expression is "(만나서) 반갑습니다."

✅ QUIZ

2. Look at the picture and fill in the blank.

안녕하세요? 김유나_____.
만나서 _____.

kim_yuna 팔로우
게시물 30   팔로워 2,078   팔로우 696
김유나

만나서 반가워요. It's nice to meet you.

02 다니엘 하임이에요

03 저는 독일 사람이에요
I'm German

A 저는 독일 사람이에요. I'm German.

 N은/는

- "은/는" is placed after the noun that is the topic of the sentence. "는" is used when there is no batchim on the noun's final syllable.
- "은" is used when the noun's final syllable has a batchim.

| 받침 ✕ + 는 | 알리사 → 알리사는 | 받침 ○ + 은 | 기욤 → 기욤은 |

Talking about nationality 1

Nationality can be expressed with "[country name] + 사람."

독일   영국   한국   + 사람

e.g. 저는 한국 사람이에요.
마이클 씨는 영국 사람이에요.

독일 Germany   사람 person   독일 사람 German (person)   영국 United Kingdom(U.K.)
영국 사람 English (person)

A 마이클은 영국 사람이에요. Michael is English.

A 마이클__ 영국 사람____.

🟢 나라 이름 Country name

| 미국 | 일본 | 중국 | 인도 | 프랑스 | 베트남 |

🟢 언어 Languages

The Korean words for languages are typically formed by adding "-어" to the name of the country.

e.g. 일본어, 중국어, …

One exception is "영어" (English), which derives from "영국 + -어."

QUIZ

1. Match the Korean word to its English equivalent.

1) 영국 •   • a. Germany

2) 독일 •   • b. U.K.

2. Match the expressions with the correct form of "은/는."

1) 저 •

2) 기욤 •   • a. 은

3) 마이클 •   • b. 는

03 저는 독일 사람이에요

A 알리사 씨는 독일 사람이에요? Is Alisa German?
B 네, 독일 사람이에요. Yes, she's German.

💡 Interrogatives

To turn a declarative sentence into an interrogative one (that is, a question), simply add a question mark and end the sentence with rising intonation.

e.g. 알리사 씨는 독일 사람이에요. ↘
      알리사 씨는 독일 사람이에요? ↗

💡 네

When the information the other person is asking about is correct, respond with "네."

e.g. A: 독일 사람이에요?   B: 네, 독일 사람이에요.

➕ Omitting the subject

When the subject of a Korean sentence is obvious, it can be omitted.

e.g. A: 알리사 씨는 독일 사람이에요?
      B: 네, 저는 독일 사람이에요.
         = 네, (저는) 독일 사람이에요.

네 yes   그래요? Is that so?   아니요 no

A 마이클은 독일 사람이에요? Is Michael German?
B 아니요, 마이클은 영국 사람이에요. No, Michael is English.

 아니요

When the information the other person is asking about is incorrect, respond with "아니요."

e.g. A: 독일 사람이에요?   B: 아니요, 영국 사람이에요.

Culture

당신 / 너 You

The most literal Korean equivalents to the English second-person pronoun "you" are "당신" and "너." However, "당신" is generally used by married couples or people who are quarreling angrily, while "너" is only used in the casual speech style to a close friend or someone who is younger or lower in rank. So how exactly are you supposed to refer to the other person when asking a question in Korean? The subject of the sentence is generally omitted in such cases. Of course, eye contact or other nonverbal techniques should still be used to ensure the other person knows they are being asked a question.

QUIZ

3. Read the following and respond with "네" or "아니요."

1) A: 마이클 씨는 캐나다 사람이에요?
   B: _____, 저는 캐나다 사람이에요.

2) A: 유나 씨는 일본 사람이에요?
   B: _____, 한국 사람이에요.

04 저는 학생이 아니에요
I'm Not a Student

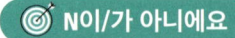 N이/가 아니에요

 A 다니엘 씨는 직업이 뭐예요? What is your job, Daniel?
B 기자예요. I'm a reporter.

다니엘 씨는 _____이 뭐예요? A

B _____예요.

➕ **직업이 뭐예요?** What is your job?

When asking about someone's job, the correct expression to use is, "직업이 뭐예요?"

➕ **직업** Jobs

기자 회사원 학생 의사
가수 배우 연구원 선생님

직업 job   기자 reporter   회사원 office worker   학생 student   의사 doctor   가수 singer
배우 actor   연구원 researcher   선생님 teacher

A 유나 씨는 직업이 뭐예요? What is your job, Yu-na?
B 저는 회사원이에요. I'm an office worker.

 Listen to the recording and respond with your own information.

직업이 뭐예요?

QUIZ

1. Look at the picture and complete the sentence.

1)  마이클 씨는 _____.

2) 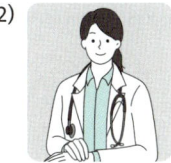 마리아 씨는 _____.

3)  수진 씨는 _____.

A 마이클 씨는 기자예요? Are you a reporter, Michael?
B 아니요, 저는 기자가 아니에요. No, I'm not a reporter.

N이/가 아니에요

This is used to state that the subject does not have the quality of N. "가" is placed after a noun without a batchim, and "이" is placed after a noun with a batchim.

받침 ✕	+ 가 아니에요	가수가 아니에요
받침 ○	+ 이 아니에요	학생이 아니에요

QUIZ

2. Choose the correct form of "이/가."

1) 마리아 씨는 회사원(이, 가) 아니에요. 의사예요.
2) 라라 씨는 가수(이, 가) 아니에요. 배우예요.
3) 저는 기자(이, 가) 아니에요. 학생이에요.
4) 저는 독일 사람(이, 가) 아니에요. 영국 사람이에요.

아니다 to not be (someone/something)

A 유나 씨는 학생이에요? Are you a student, Yu-na?
B 아니요, 저는 학생이 아니에요. 회사원이에요.
No, I'm not a student. I'm an office worker.

Culture

한국 학생들에게 인기 있는 직업은? Most popular careers for korean students

What are the most popular careers for Korean students? According to a recent survey, the most popular career choice among elementary school students is athlete, followed by doctor and teacher. Creators, such as YouTubers, follow closely behind. For middle and high school students, the top career choice is teacher. The second most popular career choice for middle school students is doctor and the third is police officer/investigator, while the second most popular career choice for high school students is nurse and the third is a career in the military. In addition, an increasing number of middle and high school students are choosing computer engineers and software developers as their desired career.

QUIZ

3. Match the questions with the correct answers.

1) 영우 씨는 학생이에요?　•　　　　• a) 아니요, 한국 사람이에요.

2) 수진 씨는 회사원이에요?　•　　　• b) 아니요, 회사원이 아니에요.

3) 유나 씨는 중국 사람이에요?　•　　• c) 아니요, 회사원이에요.

05 지금 공부해요
I'm Studying Right Now

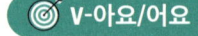

A 미나는 자요? Is Mi-na sleeping?
B 네, 자요. Yes, she is.

B 네, _____.

미나는 _____? A

💡 V + -아요/어요

This expresses present-tense action in an informal situation.

❶ V + -아요
When the verb's final vowel is "ㅏ" or "ㅗ," "-아요" comes at the end.

e.g. 사다 + -아요 → 사요   보다 + -아요 → 봐요

➕ **동사 (1)** Verbs (1)

사다 → 사요   자다 → 자요   만나다 → 만나요   오다 → 와요   보다 → 봐요

사다 to buy   자다 to sleep   만나다 to meet   오다 to come   보다 to see

A 지금 공부해요? Are you studying right now?
B 네, 공부해요. Yes, I am.

A 지금 _____?
B 네, _____.

❷ -하다 ➡ -해요

When the verb ends in "-하다," "-해요" comes at the end.

e.g. 공부하다 → 공부해요   일하다 → 일해요

➕ 동사 (2) Verbs (2)

공부하다 → 공부해요   일하다 → 일해요   운동하다 → 운동해요

🔍 QUIZ

1. Look at the picture and use "-아요/어요" to complete the dialogue.

1)    A: 미나는 뭐 해요?
   B: _____.

2)    A: 지금 뭐 해요?
   B: _____.

지금 (right) now   뭐 what   공부하다 to study   일하다 to work   운동하다 to exercise

A 지금 뭐 해요? What are you doing right now?
B 밥 먹어요. I'm eating a meal.

❸ V + -어요 (1)

When the verb's final vowel is not "ㅏ" or "ㅗ" and when the verb does not end in "-하다," "-어요" comes at the end.

e.g. 먹다 + -어요 → 먹어요   배우다 + -어요 → 배워요

동사(3) Verbs (3)

먹다 → 먹어요   배우다 → 배워요   읽다 → 읽어요   쉬다 → 쉬어요   주다 → 줘요

 **발음** Pronunciation

When the batchim "ㄺ" is followed by a consonant other than "ㄱ", only "ㄱ" is pronounced. When the batchim "ㄺ" is followed by a vowel, "ㄹ" is pronounced as the batchim and "ㄱ" is pronounced with the following vowel.

e.g. 읽다 [익따]   읽어요 [일거요]

밥 rice, a meal   먹다 to eat   배우다 to learn   읽다 to read   쉬다 to rest   주다 to give

A 지금 뭐 해요? What are you doing right now?
B 커피 마셔요. I'm drinking coffee.

지금 뭐 _____ ? A

B 커피 _____ .

❹ V + -어요 (2)

When the final vowel in the verb is " ㅣ," "-여요" comes at the end.

e.g. 마시다 → 마셔요   가르치다 → 가르쳐요

Culture

선생님 The cultral meaning of "선생님" in Korea

The basic meaning of "선생님" is someone who teaches students (i.e., a teacher). But in Korea, the word can also serve as a respectful form of address. Foreigners who aren't aware of that sometimes ask why there are so many teachers in Korea. Since "선생님" is also a respectful way of referring to someone, it's important to remember that being called "선생님" doesn't necessarily mean someone is a teacher.

QUIZ

2. Look at the picture and use "-아요/어요" to complete the dialogue.

1)

A: 지금 뭐 해요?

B: _____ .

2)

A: 지금 뭐 해요?

B: _____ .

3)

A: 지금 뭐 해요?

B: _____ .

4)

A: 지금 뭐 해요?

B: _____ .

커피 coffee   마시다 to drink   가르치다 to teach   기다리다 to wait

06 커피를 좋아해요
I Like Coffee

A 커피를 좋아해요? Do you like coffee?
B 네, 좋아해요. Yes, I do.

 **N을/를**

"을/를" is placed after a noun to show that it's the object of the sentence. "를" is used when the noun doesn't have a batchim, and "을" is used when it does. In the spoken language, "을/를" may be omitted.

받침 X	+ 를	커피를
받침 O	+ 을	아이스크림을

 **발음** Pronunciation

When followed by a vowel, batchim (the final consonant) "ㅎ" is silent.

 좋아해요 [조아해요]
넣어요 [너어요]

커피 coffee   좋아하다 to like   아이스크림 ice cream

A 아이스크림을 좋아해요? Do you like ice cream?
B 네, 아주 좋아해요. Yes, I like it very much.

➕ 음식, 음료 Food and beverages

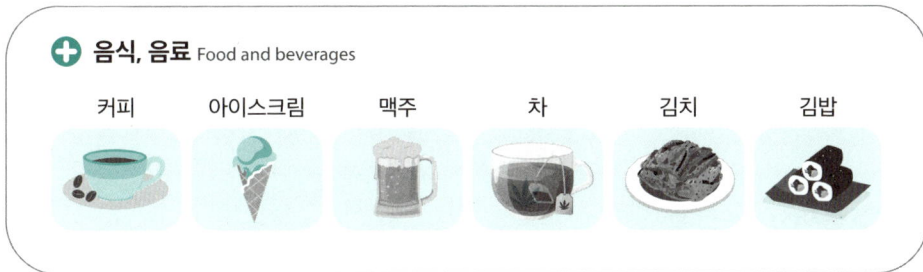

커피 아이스크림 맥주 차 김치 김밥

✅UIZ

1. Mark the correct form of "을/를."

1) 아이스크림 (을, 를) 좋아해요.

2) 저는 차 (을, 를) 좋아해요.

3) 저는 김치 (을, 를) 좋아해요.

4) 마이클은 김밥 (을, 를) 좋아해요.

아주 very   맥주 beer   차 tea   김치 kimchi   김밥 gimbap

A 지금 뭐 해요? What are you doing right now?
B 밥을 먹어요. I'm eating a meal.

 N을/를

"뭐를" can be shortened to "뭘," and further shortened to "뭐."

e.g. 뭐를 → 뭘 → 뭐(를)

운동하다 to exercise   청소하다 to clean   일하다 to work   요리하다 to cook

A 유나 씨는 지금 뭐 해요? What are you doing right now, Yu-na?
B 공부를 해요. I'm studying.

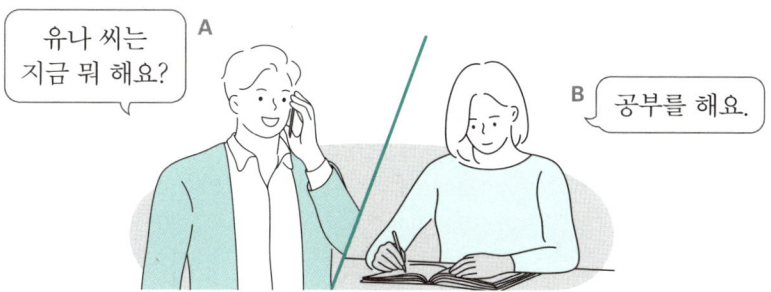

 Listen to the recording and respond with your own information.

지금 뭘 해요?

 **N하다**

In the case of verbs that take the form "N+하다," the object particle "을/를" can be placed at the end of the noun.

 공부해요 = 공부를 해요   운동해요 = 운동을 해요

QUIZ

2. What are they doing right now? Look at the picture and complete the sentence.

1)  김밥_____.

2)  운동_____.

3)  맥주_____.

4)  요리_____.

07 고기를 안 먹어요
I Don't Eat Meat

A 고기를 먹어요? Do you eat meat?
B 아니요, 고기를 안 먹어요. No, I don't.

고기를 _____? A

B 아니요, 고기를 ___ ___.

"안" is written before the verb to make the sentence negative in meaning.

e.g. 먹어요 → **안** 먹어요
　　 마셔요 → **안** 마셔요

음식 이름 Food names

소고기　돼지고기　닭고기　생선　떡볶이　김치

고기 meat　소고기 beef　돼지고기 pork　닭고기 chicken　생선 fish　떡볶이 tteokbokki
김치 kimchi

A 뭐를 안 먹어요? What don't you eat?
B 저는 닭고기를 안 먹어요. I don't eat chicken.

발음 Pronunciation

The double batchim "ㄺ" is pronounced [ㄱ] at the end of a word or in front of a consonant. That means "닭고기" is pronounced [닥꼬기].

QUIZ

1. Answer the question using one of the items depicted below.

1)

비빔밥 불고기 냉면
김밥 떡볶이 김치

A: 뭐를 안 먹어요?
B: 저는 _____.

2)

녹차 콜라 우유
주스 커피 맥주

A: 뭐를 안 마셔요?
B: 저는 _____.

뭐 what   비빔밥 bibimbap   불고기 bulgogi   냉면 naengmyeon   김밥 gimbap
녹차 green tea   콜라 cola   우유 milk   주스 juice   커피 coffee   맥주 beer

A 일본어를 공부해요? Do you study Japanese?
B 아니요, 일본어를 공부 안 해요. No, I don't study Japanese.

안 V

In the case of verbs that take the form "N + 하다," such as "공부하다" and "일하다," "안" must be written before "하다."

e.g. 공부해요. → 공부 **안** 해요.
      운동해요. → 운동 **안** 해요.

QUIZ

2. Read the dialogue and provide the correct answer.

1) A: 김치를 먹어요?
   B: 아니요, _____.

2) A: 운동해요?
   B: 아니요, _____.

3) A: 커피를 마셔요?
   B: 아니요, _____.

4) A: 일본어를 공부해요?
   B: 아니요, _____.

5) A: 고기를 좋아해요?
   B: 아니요, _____.

A 커피를 좋아해요? Do you like coffee?
B 아니요, 커피를 안 좋아해요. No, I don't like coffee.

A 커피를 _____?
B 아니요, _____.

 안 V

"좋아하다" is not a verb of the form "N + 하다," so the negative form of "좋아해요" is "안 좋아해요," not "좋아 안 해요."

e.g. 고기를 **안** 좋아해요.

Culture

물냉면 / 비빔냉면 Mul-naengmyeon / Bibim-naengmyeon

Naengmyeon is a beloved Korean dish that is especially popular in the summer. There are two basic types: buckwheat noodles served in a cold broth are called mul-naengmyeon, while noodles mixed in a thick sauce without any broth are called bibim-naengmyeon ("bibim" means "mixing up"). Bibim-naengmyeon is rather spicy because of the chili pepper in the sauce. Koreans generally add vinegar and mustard to their naengmyeon. Mul-naengmyeon can be abbreviated to "mul-naeng," and bibim-naengmyeon to "bi-naeng." The chewy naengmyeon noodles are sometimes chopped up with scissors before eating. Don't worry, though: those scissors are only used with food.

QUIZ

3. Answer the following questions by marking "네/아니요."

1) 고기를 먹어요?   네 ☐ 아니요 ☐   2) 맥주를 마셔요?   네 ☐ 아니요 ☐
3) 운동해요?   네 ☐ 아니요 ☐   4) 콜라를 좋아해요? 네 ☐ 아니요 ☐

08 집에 가요
I'm Going Home

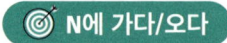 N에 가다/오다

A 집에 가요? Are you going home?
B 네, 집에 가요. Yes, I am.

 N에 가다/오다

When placed after a noun of location, this expresses movement toward a destination.

받침 ✕	+ 에 가다	학교에 가요
받침 ○		집에 가요

발음 Pronunciation

The letters "ㄱ, ㄷ, ㅂ, ㅅ, ㅈ" are glottalized as "ㄲ, ㄸ, ㅃ, ㅆ, ㅉ" when they come after a batchim pronounced [ㄱ], [ㄷ], or [ㅂ].

e.g. 학교 [학꾜]   식당 [식땅]

집 home, house   가다 to go

A 집에 가요? Are you going home?
B 아니요, 집에 안 가요. 식당에 가요. 오늘 친구를 만나요.
No, I'm not. I'm going to a restaurant. I'm going to meet a friend today.

가다 vs. 오다

"가다" indicates movement away from the speaker's current location, while "오다" indicates movement toward the speaker's current location.

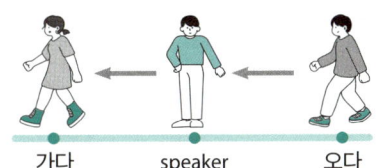

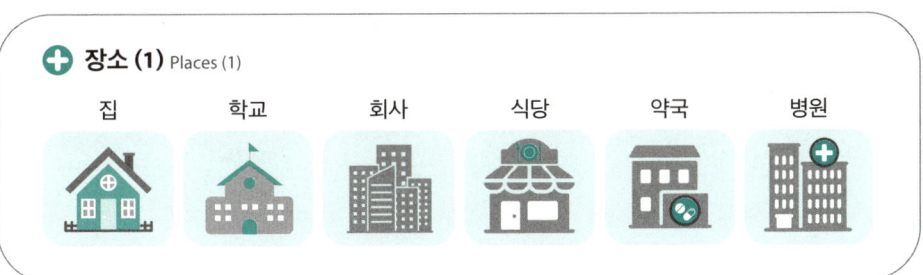

장소 (1) Places (1)

집 학교 회사 식당 약국 병원

식당 restaurant   오늘 today   친구 friend   학교 school   회사 company   약국 pharmacy
병원 hospital

A 어디에 가요? Where are you going?
B 식당에 가요. I'm going to a restaurant.

💡 어디에 가요?

When asking someone where they're going, the particle "에" is added to the word "어디" (where), giving the question "어디에 가요?" In daily conversation, the particle "에" can be left off.

➕ 장소 (2) Places (2)

백화점   카페   영화관   편의점   공원   공항

어디 where   백화점 department store   카페 cafe   영화관 movie theater
편의점 convenience store   공원 park   공항 airport

A 내일 어디에 가요? Where are you going tomorrow?
B 백화점에 가요. I'm going to a department store.

A 내일 _____ 가요?
B _____ 가요.

🎤 Listen to the recording and respond with your own information.

내일 어디에 가요?

✓UIZ

1. Look at the picture and complete the dialogue.

 1) A: 학교에 가요?
B: 네, _____.

 2) A: 회사에 가요?
B: 네, _____.

 3) A: 집에 가요?
B: 네, _____.

 4) A: 병원에 가요?
B: 네, _____.

2. Match each question with the appropriate answer.

1) 어디에 가요? •　　　　• a) 아니요, 영화관에 가요.
2) 내일 영화를 봐요?　•　　　　• b) 영국 사람이에요.
3) 어느 나라 사람이에요?　•　　　　• c) 아니요, 영화를 안 봐요.
4) 지금 백화점에 가요?　•　　　　• d) 영화관에 가요.

09 집에서 밥을 먹어요
I Eat Meals at Home

A 어디에서 운동해요? Where do you exercise?
B 공원에서 운동해요. I exercise at the park.

A _____ 운동해요?
B _____ 운동해요.

The particle "에서" is written after a noun of location to indicate where a certain action is taking place.

	+ 에서	
받침 ✕		카페에서
받침 ○		집에서

 e.g. 카페에서 친구를 만나요.
집에서 밥을 먹어요.

Culture

한국의 카페 Korea's cafe

Visitors to a Korean cafe will find not only people drinking coffee but also quite a few people studying. If you leave your bag and phone on the table to visit the restroom, they're very unlikely to disappear while you're away. While at a cafe, you can access Wi-Fi and charge your laptop or mobile phone for free. Are cafes like that back in your home country?

A 어디에서 공부해요? Where do you study?
B 학교에서 공부해요. I study at school.

___ 공부해요? A

B ___ 공부해요.

QUIZ

1. Fill in each blank with the correct particle.

에 / 에서

1) 조나단은 영화관(　　) 영화를 봐요.
2) 미나는 백화점(　　) 가요.
3) 나는 집(　　) 쉬어요.
4) 마이클 씨는 회사(　　) 일해요.

A 어디에서 일해요? Where do you work?
B 여기에서 일해요. I work here.

여기, 저기

- "여기" is used to indicate a place that is close to the speaker.
  - e.g. 미나 씨는 여기에서 공부해요.

- "저기" is used to indicate a place that is far from both the speaker and the listener.
  - e.g. 토니 씨는 저기에서 운동해요.

QUIZ

2. Complete each dialogue with one of the following sentences.

- 공원에서 만나요
- 커피를 좋아해요
- 집에서 공부해요
- 카페에 가요

1) A: 어디에 가요?
   B: _____.

2) A: 어디에서 친구를 만나요?
   B: _____.

3) A: 지금 뭐 해요?
   B: _____.

여기 here   저기 over there

A 어디서 커피를 마셔요? Where do you drink coffee?
B 저기서 마셔요. I drink coffee over there.

💡 어디서, 여기서, 저기서

- "어디에서," which combines the interrogative word "어디" (where) with the particle "에서," can be abbreviated as "어디서." In the same way, "여기에서" can be abbreviated as "여기서" and "저기에서" as "저기서." This kind of abbreviation is especially common in speech.

| 어디에서 = 어디서 | 여기에서 = 여기서 | 저기에서 = 저기서 |

- However, the particle "에서" cannot be abbreviated when combined with a noun of location.

| 학교에서 = 학교서(X) |

10 오늘 수업이 없어요
I Don't Have Class Today

A 우산이 있어요? Do you have an umbrella?
B 네, 있어요. Yes, I do.

N이/가 있다

"이/가 있어요" indicates that the subject of the sentence has the thing, object, or person that comes before "이/가." "가" is used when the noun doesn't end in a batchim and "이" is used when it does. "이/가" can be omitted in speech.

| 받침 X + 가 있다 | 휴지가 있어요 | 받침 O + 이 있다 | 우산이 있어요 |

QUIZ

1. Choose the correct particle from "이/가."

1) 볼펜(이, 가) 있어요.
2) 지우개(이, 가) 있어요?
3) 지금 돈(이, 가) 있어요?
4) 저는 차(이, 가) 있어요.

우산 umbrella   있다 to have, to be (somewhere)   차 car

A 휴지가 있어요? Do you have any tissues?
B 네, 여기 있어요. Yes, here you are.

A 휴지____ ____?

B 네, 여기 있어요.

물건 Things

| 볼펜 | 지우개 | 돈 | 모자 | 휴대폰 | 차 |

여기 있어요 Here you are

"여기 있어요" is the expression used when handing over an item, such as money, to another person.

Culture

화장실 밖에서도 쓰는 화장지 Toilet paper beyond the bathroom

In Korea, toilet paper is sometimes used outside the bathroom as well. You might occasionally see people using it to blow their nose or wipe their mouth, including in casual places like restaurants.

휴지 toilet paper   여기 here   볼펜 ballpoint pen   지우개 eraser   돈 money   모자 hat
휴대폰 mobile phone

A 우산이 있어요? Do you have an umbrella?
B 아니요, 없어요. No, I don't.

N이/가 없다

"없다" is the opposite of "있다." "이/가 없어요" indicates that the subject of the sentence does not have the thing, object, or person that comes before "이/가."

 **발음** Pronunciation

When batchim "ㅄ" is followed by a consonant, only [ㅂ] is pronounced. When it is followed by a vowel, [ㅂ] is pronounced as the batchim and [ㅅ] is pronounced with the following vowel.

e.g. 없다 [업따]   없어요 [업써요]

➕ **일, 일정** Work and schedule

시간   약속   숙제   시험   일

없다 to not have   수업 class   시간 time   약속 appointment   숙제 homework   시험 test
일 work

A 내일 학교에 가요? Are you going to school tomorrow?
B 아니요, 안 가요. 내일 수업이 없어요. No, I'm not. I don't have class tomorrow.

 Listen to the recording and respond with your own information.

오늘 약속이 있어요?

QUIZ

2. Look at the picture and complete the sentence.

1)
숙제가 _____.

2)
오늘 약속이 _____.

3)
지금 시간이 _____.

4)
저는 차가 _____.

10 오늘 수업이 없어요 53

11 물냉면 주세요
I Would Like Some Mul-Naengmyeon

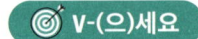 V-(으)세요

 A 어서 오세요. Come on in!
B 여기 앉으세요. Please take a seat.

 V-(으)세요

A verb conjugated with "-(으)세요" is used to make a request or give an order.

| 받침 ✕ | -세요 | 오다 → 오세요 |
| 받침 〇 | -으세요 | 읽다 → 읽으세요 |

➕ 어서 오세요 Come on in
"어서 오세요" is a generic greeting used to welcome guests into a store or restaurant.

 발음 Pronunciation

"앉으세요" is pronounced as [안즈세요].

e.g. 앉으세요 [안즈세요]

A 뭐 드릴까요? What can I get for you today?
B 물냉면 주세요. I would like some mul-naengmyeon.

뭐 드릴까요? What can I get for you today?

"뭐 드릴까요?" (literally meaning "what shall I give you?") is the expression used by store or restaurant staff to ask customers what they need. The typical response takes the form "NOUN 주세요."

QUIZ

1. Look at the picture and conjugate each verb using "-(으)세요."

보다	읽다	운동하다	쉬다	요리하다	앉다
		운동하세요			

11 물냉면 주세요

A 물 좀 주세요. Can I have some water?
B 네, 잠깐만 기다리세요. Yes, please wait just a moment.

 좀 + V

- "좀" is placed before a verb to soften a request.

    e.g. 쉬세요 → 좀 쉬세요.

- There are certain items at restaurants (such as menus, utensils, and napkins) that can be requested at no cost. When requesting one of these items, it is courteous to use the word "좀."

    e.g. 메뉴 주세요. → 메뉴 좀 주세요.

- But "좀" is typically not used when ordering something you will have to pay for.

    e.g. 비빔밥 좀 주세요. (X)   비빔밥 주세요. (O)

Culture

반찬 Side dishes

When eating out in Korea, 반찬 (side dishes) are served alongside the main entrees. In the case of hanjeongsik, a full-course meal consisting of several traditional dishes, guests may be served ten or more side dishes. Korean restaurants generally don't charge for such side dishes, including kimchi. If you run low on side dishes during your meal, you can ask for more at no cost.

A 김치 좀 더 주세요. Can I have some more kimchi?
B 네, 잠깐만 기다리세요. Yes, please wait just a moment.

B 네, 잠깐만 _____.

A 김치 좀 _____.

➕ **더 주세요** More, please

This expression is used when asking for more of something.

e.g. 밥 더 주세요.   돈 좀 더 주세요.

✅UIZ

2. Look at the picture and use either "주세요" or "좀 주세요" to request each item at a restaurant.

커피   숟가락   비빔밥   불고기
메뉴   김밥   김치   물

더 more

11 물냉면 주세요 57

참치김밥 하나 주세요
I Would Like One Tuna Gimbap

 Numbers 1: 하나, 둘, 셋…

A 뭐 드릴까요? What can I get for you today?
B 참치김밥 하나 주세요. I would like one tuna gimbap.

 **Numbers 1**

Korean basically has two kinds of numbers: pure Korean numbers and Sino-Korean numbers (the latter being based on Chinese characters). Pure Korean numbers (하나, 둘, 셋, 넷, etc.) are used to count people or objects. Particular attention should be paid to word order here: the thing you are counting comes first, and the number comes second.

e.g. 사과 하나를 사요.   사과 하나를 주세요.

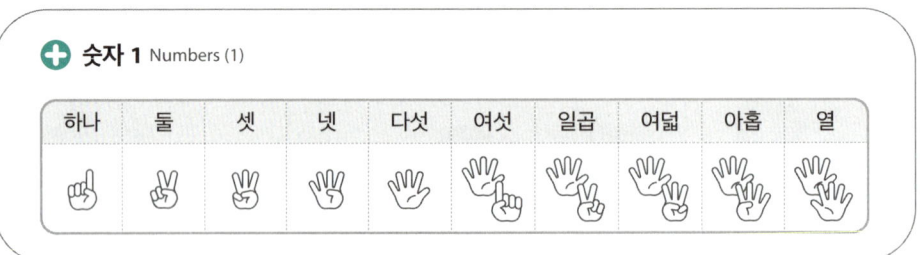

참치김밥 tuna gimbap

A 저기요. Excuse me!
B 뭐 드릴까요? What would you like today?
A 비빔밥 둘 주세요. I would like two bowls of bibimbap.

➕ 저기요 Excuse me

"저기요" can be used to politely get the attention of a waiter at a restaurant or café or call them to your table.

QUIZ

1. Write down how many things you see in each picture.

1)
콜라 _____

2)
물냉면 _____

3)
_____

4)
_____

A 뭐 드시겠어요? What would you like to have today?
B 비빔밥 하나 주세요. I would like one bowl of bibimbap.

➕ **뭐 드시겠어요?** What would you like to have?

Along with "뭐 드릴까요?," another way for waiters to take an order is to ask "뭐 드시겠어요?" This expression uses the verb "드시다," an honorific form of "먹다." Honorific expressions such as "뭐 드시겠어요?" are used with the elderly and people of high social status.

Culture

한국에서 채식하기 Being a vegetarian in Korea

The easiest dishes for vegetarians to find in Korea are bibimbap and veggie gimbap. But since even those dishes sometimes include animal-based ingredients such as eggs, ham, or fish cake, vegetarians who want to play it safe should provide the following information when making an order: "저는 채식주의자예요" (I'm a vegetarian), "저는 고기를 안 먹어요" (I don't eat meat), and "고기는 빼 주세요" (please hold the meat). One place where vegetarians can dine without any worries about animal products is a cafeteria at a Buddhist temple or a restaurant specializing in temple cuisine. Given the Buddhist prohibition against killing living creatures, you can rest assured that the wide range of delicious dishes served up there are strictly vegetarian.

A 뭐 드시겠어요? What would you like to have today?
B 비빔밥 하나 주세요. 달걀은 빼 주세요.
I would like one bowl of bibimbap, but please hold the eggs.

➕ **N은/는 빼 주세요** Hold the N, please

This expression is used at a restaurant to request that a particular ingredient be "held," or left off your food or drink order.

e.g. 달걀은 빼 주세요.   양파는 빼 주세요.

QUIZ

2. Look at the picture and complete the sentence.

1) 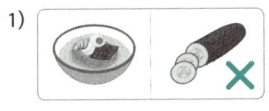 _____ 하나 주세요.   오이는 빼 주세요.

2)  햄버거 ____ ____.   ____는 빼 주세요.

3)  야채김밥 ____ ____.   ____은 빼 주세요.

달걀 egg   양파 onion   야채김밥 veggie gimbap

13 맥주 두 병하고 소주 한 병 주세요
Two Bottles of Beer and One Bottle of Soju, Please

 N하고 N

A 뭐 드릴까요? What would you like to have today?
B 물냉면 한 그릇 주세요. I would like one bowl of mul-naengmyeon.

A: _____ 드릴까요?
B: 물냉면 _____ _____ 주세요.

Measure words

개, 병, 잔, and 그릇 are examples of measure words, or counters, which are used to count the number of something.

그릇 bowl   잔 cup, glass   개 general counting unit   병 bottle

A 뭐 드릴까요? What can I get for you today?
B 커피 세 잔 주세요. I would like three cups of coffee.

뭐 _____ ?
B 커피 _____ 주세요.

한, 두, 세, 네…

- The numeral determiner (수 관형사) must be used along with a measure word (개, 병, 잔, 그릇) when counting an object. The numeral determiners, which are sometimes slightly different from the regular numbers, are listed below.

1	2	3	4	5	6	7	8	9	10	11
하나	둘	셋	넷	다섯	여섯	일곱	여덟	아홉	열	열하나
한 개	두 개	세 개	네 개	다섯 개	여섯 개	일곱 개	여덟 개	아홉 개	열 개	열한 개

- The word order is as follows: name of the object + numeral determiner + measure word.

  e.g. 사과 한 개   맥주 두 병   커피 세 잔   냉면 한 그릇

QUIZ

1. Try ordering what you see in the picture.

커피 3

사과 5

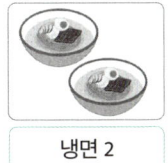
냉면 2

맥주 4

13 맥주 두 병하고 소주 한 병 주세요

A 맥주 두 병하고 소주 한 병 주세요.
Two bottles of beer and one bottle of soju, please.

B 네, 잠깐만 기다리세요. Yes, please wait just a moment.

 N하고 N

The conjunction "하고" is used to link two or more nouns. The word is the same regardless of whether the preceding noun has a batchim.

받침 ✕	+ 하고	김치하고
받침 ○		밥하고

Culture

술 마실 때 예절 Drinking etiquette

There are a lot of different customs to remember in Korea, including the ones connected with drinking alcohol. When drinking with an older individual, you should turn your head to the side while taking a drink. But that's only required for alcohol, not water. Another point to remember is that Koreans don't like to refill a glass of alcohol until it's empty (doing so is called "첨잔"). If you'd like to pour more alcohol for your drinking partner, encourage them to empty their glass first. And when several people are drinking together, you shouldn't pour yourself alcohol. Going out for a drink in Korea involves some complicated customs, doesn't it? How are things in your home country?

햄버거 hamburger   샌드위치 sandwich

A 여기요. 빵 한 개하고 커피 한 잔하고 주스 한 병 주세요.
Excuse me! I would like one piece of bread, one cup of coffee, and one bottle of juice.

B 네, 알겠습니다. OK, got it.

N과/와 N

"과/와" mean the same thing as "하고," but these conjunctions are more frequently used in writing than in speaking.

| 받침 X + 와 | 사과와 |

| 받침 O + 과 | 비빔밥과 |

➕ **여기요** Excuse me

"여기요" is another expression that can be used to call over a restaurant server or store attendant.

➕ **알겠습니다** Understood

"알겠습니다" is a polite way of indicating that you've understood what was said to you.

QUIZ

2. Write down what you see in each picture.

1) 사과 4 ➕ 물 1
_____ 주세요.

2) 샌드위치 8 ➕ 콜라 9
_____ 주세요.

14 천 원이에요
It's 1,000 Won

Numbers 2: 일, 이, 삼…

A 얼마예요? How much is it?
B 천 원이에요. It's 1,000 won.

A ___예요?
B ___ 원이에요.

Numbers 2

Sino-Korean numbers (일, 이, 삼, 사, etc.) are most notably used in prices, dates, and phone numbers.

e.g. 일 달러 / 오 유로 / 십 원

숫자 2 Numbers (2)

1	2	3	4	5	6	7	8	9	10
일	이	삼	사	오	육	칠	팔	구	십

…	20	30	40	50	60	70	80	90	100
	이십	삼십	사십	오십	육십	칠십	팔십	구십	백

10	100	1,000	10,000	100,000	1,000,000
십	백	천	만	십만	백만

A 얼마예요? How much is it?
B 만 원이에요. It's 10,000 won.

 **발음** Pronunciation

Batchim "ㅂ" and "ㄱ" are both pronounced differently before "ㅁ," with "ㅂ" pronounced as [ㅁ] and "ㄱ" pronounced as [ㅇ]. For that reason, "십만" is pronounced as [심만] and "백만" is pronounced as [뱅만].

QUIZ

1. Write down each price in Hangul.

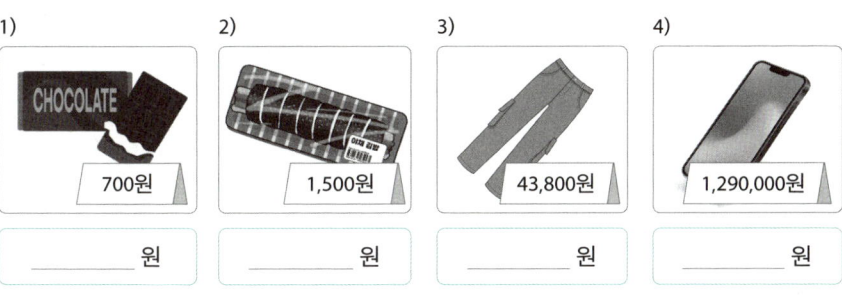

얼마 how much   원 won (the Korean currency)   달러 dollar   유로 euro

A 이거 얼마예요? How much is this?
B 이만 원이에요. It's 20,000 won.

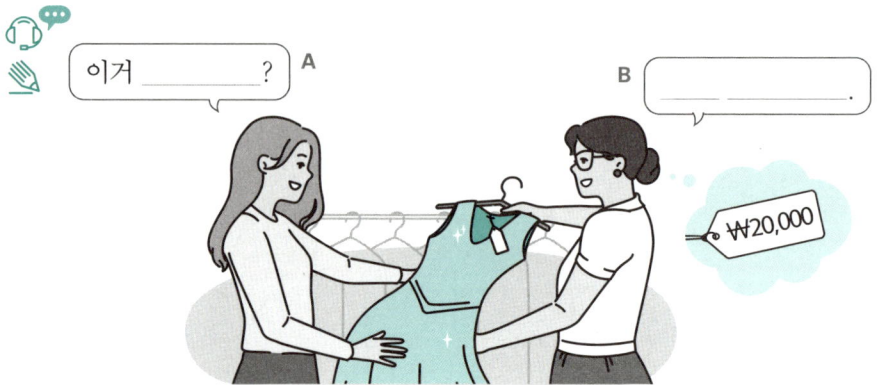

이거, 그거, 저거

"이거," "그거," and "저거" refer to something being pointed at either figuratively or literally. "이거" is used when the object in question is close to the speaker, "그거" is used when the object is close to the listener, and "저거" is used when the object is far from both the speaker and the listener.

Culture

한국의 화폐 단위 The Korean currency

The Korean currency is called "원" (won), which takes the currency symbol "₩." The money currently in circulation consists of 10 won, 50 won, 100 won, and 500 won coins and 1,000 won, 5,000 won, 10,000 won, and 50,000 won bills. Both coins and bills depict significant figures and objects from Korean history.

A 이거 하나에 얼마예요? How much is it for one of these?
B 천 원이에요. It's 1,000 won.

이거 _____ 얼마예요? A

B _____.

➕ **하나에 얼마예요?** How much for one?

This expression is used when asking about the price per item. Instead of "하나에" (meaning "per item"), you can also use the numeral determiner and measure word together, as in the following phrases: "한 개에," "한 병에," and "한 잔에."

QUIZ

2. Match each question with the most appropriate answer.

1) 뭐 드릴까요?　　•　　　　• a) 하나에 천 원이에요.

2) 물냉면이 있어요?　•　　　　• b) 네, 있어요.

3) 이거 얼마예요?　•　　　　• c) 사과 열 개 주세요.

이거 this　　하나에 per item

15 양념치킨이 맛있어요
Yangnyeom Chicken Tastes Good

 N이/가 A-아요/어요

A 비빔밥이 맛있어요? Does the bibimbap taste good?
B 네, 맛있어요. Yes, it does.

비빔밥___ ___? A

B 네, ___.

N이/가 A-아요/어요

This is used to describe the condition or nature of the noun. In this case, the subject particle "이/가" is placed after the noun that the adjective is modifying.

| 받침 X + 가 | 불고기 + 가 → 불고기가 | 받침 O + 이 | 비빔밥 + 이 → 비빔밥이 |

- When the adjective's last vowel is "ㅏ, ㅗ," "-아요" is placed at the end.
- When the adjective ends in "-하다," "-해요" is placed at the end.
- When the adjective's last vowel is not "ㅏ, ㅗ" and it doesn't end in "-하다," "-어요" is placed at the end.

ㅏ, ㅗ	-하다	in all other cases
싸다 + -아요 → 싸요	따뜻하다 → 따뜻해요	맛있다 + -어요 → 맛있어요
좋다 + -아요 → 좋아요	시원하다 → 시원해요	맛없다 + -어요 → 맛없어요

맛있다 to taste good   맛없다 to taste bad   싸다 to be cheap   좋다 to be good
따뜻하다 to be warm   시원하다 to be cool, to be refreshing

A 케이크가 맛있어요? Does the cake taste good?
B 아니요, 맛없어요. No, it doesn't.

A 케이크_____?   B 아니요, _____.

안 A

- "안" is written before an adjective to make a negative sentence.

  e.g. 좋아요. → 안 좋아요   따뜻하다 → 안 따뜻해요

- Note that "맛없어요" (to taste bad) is often used as the negative form of "맛있어요" (to taste good).

 **발음** Pronunciation

"맛있다" is technically pronounced [마딛따], but it can also be pronounced [마싣따]. In fact, Koreans typically pronounce it the second way, as [마싣따]. In contrast, "맛없다" is only pronounced [마덥따], and [마섭따] is incorrect. Take note of how you pronounce these two words.

QUIZ

1. Look at the picture and complete the sentence.

1) 피자 / 맛있다

2) 코트 / 따뜻하다

3) 김밥 / 싸다

피자(이/가) _____.   코트(이/가) _____.   김밥(이/가) _____.

15 양념치킨이 맛있어요

A 뭐가 맛있어요? What tastes good here?
B 양념치킨이 아주 맛있어요. The yangnyeom chicken tastes very good.
A 그럼 양념치킨 주세요. In that case, I would like some yangnyeom chicken.

➕ 아주 Very

- When you want to emphasize an adjective, "아주" (very) or "정말" (really) can be placed in front of the adjective.
  - e.g. 맛있어요 → 아주 맛있어요 / 정말 맛있어요

- "너무" can also be used to emphasize an adjective, but it's often used with adjectives that have a negative meaning.
  - e.g. 비싸요 → 너무 비싸요   맛없어요 → 너무 맛없어요

 QUIZ

2. Look at the pictures and answer each question appropriately.

뭐가 맛있어요?
뭐가 좋아요?
뭐가 맛없어요?
뭐가 시원해요?
뭐가 싸요?

A 맥주가 시원해요? Is the beer refreshing?
B 네, 맥주가 정말 시원해요. Yes, it's very refreshing.

A 맥주가 _____ ?   B 네, 맥주 _____ .

QUIZ

3. Make a dialogue for each picture as shown in the example.

1) 🍗 • • a) 맛있어요
2) 🍺 • • b) 맛없어요
3) 🥣 • • c) 싸요
4) 🥗 • • d) 비싸요

냉면이 맛있어요?   네, 맛있어요.

Culture

치맥 Fried chicken and beer

치킨 (fried chicken) is one of Koreans' favorite snacks. There are two basic types: 프라이드 (plain) and 양념 (seasoned). 양념치킨 is coated with a sweet and spicy sauce, while 프라이드 치킨 is deep-fried until crispy without the sauce. If you say "반반 주세요" (half and half, please) while ordering fried chicken, you can try both kinds. Koreans often drink beer with fried chicken. The combo "치킨하고 맥주" can be shortened to "치맥." In Korea, drinking alcohol in parks and other public spaces isn't against the law. That's why people are often seen enjoying 치맥 at a baseball stadium or on the banks of the Hangang River in Seoul. As long as you're above the legal drinking age (19 years old in Korea), going out for some 치맥 is a good way to experience Korean culture.

그럼 then, in that case   비싸다 to be expensive

16 저녁에 운동을 해요
I Exercise in the Evening

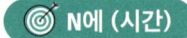 N에 (시간)

A 운동을 해요? Do you exercise?
B 네, 저는 저녁에 운동을 해요. Yes, I exercise in the evening.

A 운동을 해요?
B 네, 저는 _____ 운동을 해요.

N에 (시간) 1

The particle "에" is placed after a noun of time to express when something takes place. This grammar construction works with expressions of time, days of the week, dates, seasons, and special days.

받침 X	+ 에	오후에 친구를 만나요
받침 O		오전에 친구를 만나요

시간 (1) Time (1)

아침 점심 저녁 밤 오전 오후

저녁 evening   아침 morning   보통 usually   점심 lunch time   밤 night   오전 a.m.   오후 p.m.

A 아침에 운동을 해요? Do you exercise in the morning?
   B 아니요, 저는 보통 저녁에 운동을 해요. No, I usually exercise in the evening.

A _____ 운동을 해요?
B 아니요, 저는 보통 _____ 운동을 해요.

QUIZ

1. Look at the picture and complete the sentence.

1)
_____ 일어나요.

2)
_____ 친구를 만나요.

3)
_____ 집에 가요.

4)
_____ 약속이 있어요.

A 언제 친구를 만나요? When will you meet your friend?
B 오후에 친구를 만나요. I'll meet my friend in the afternoon.

➕ 시간 (2) Time (2)

The particle "에" is not placed after the following words related to time.

e.g. 언제에 (✗), 지금에 (✗)

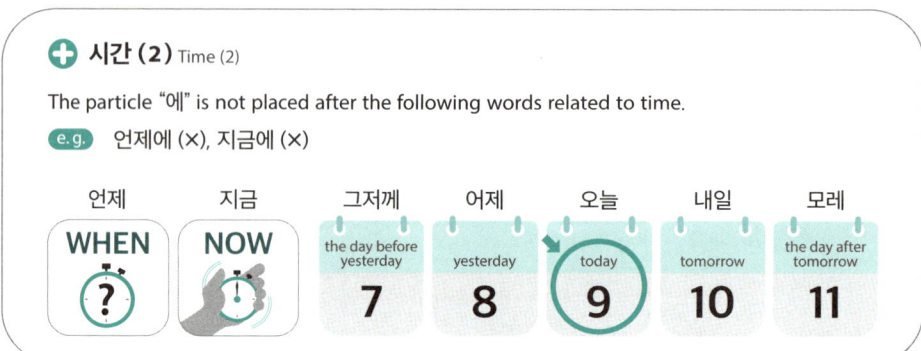

Culture

밤에도 문을 열어요 Businesses stay open late

Quite a few Korean businesses are open 24 hours a day, including not only convenience stores, but also PC rooms (PC방), karaoke rooms, and drinking establishments. There are also a lot of restaurants (some for delivery only) that stay open at night and into the early morning hours for those craving a late night snack.

언제 when   내일 tomorrow   그저께 the day before yesterday   어제 yesterday
모레 the day after tomorrow

A 언제 친구를 만나요? When will you meet your friend?
B 내일 오후에 친구를 만나요. I'll meet my friend tomorrow afternoon.

Listen to the recording and respond with your own information.

QUIZ

2. Write "에" in the blank when the particle is needed and "×" in the blank when it's not.

   1) 밤___ 친구를 만나요.
   2) 오전___ 수업이 있어요.
   3) 내일___ 오후___ 영화를 봐요.
   4) 언제___ 집___ 가요?

17 몇 시에 일어나요?
What Time Do You Get Up?

 Time (_시 _분), N에

 A 지금 몇 시예요? What time is it right now?
B 열한 시예요. It's 11 o'clock.

지금 _____ ? A
_____ 예요. B

Time (시, 분)

When talking about time, a numeral determiner (한, 두, 세, 네, etc.) is used before "시" (o'clock) and a Sino-Korean number (일, 이, 삼, 사, etc.) is used before "분" (the minute).

1	2	3	4	5	6	7	8	9	10	11	12	
한	두	세	네	다섯	여섯	일곱	여덟	아홉	열	열한	열두	+시
일	이	삼	사	오	육	칠	팔	구	십	십일	십이	+분

e.g. 지금 **여섯 시**예요.   지금 **두 시 십오 분**이에요.

➕ **몇 시** What time

The expression used to ask the time is "몇 시예요?"

e.g. A: 지금 몇 시예요?
B: 네 시 오 분이에요.

시간 time, hour   시 o'clock (when telling time)   분 the minute (when telling time)
지금 (right) now

A 지금 몇 시예요? What time is it right now?
B 오후 세 시 사십오 분이에요. It's 3:45 p.m.

지금 ___ ___? A

B ___ ___ ___ ___이에요.

➕ **30분 = 반** 30 minutes = half

"30분" (30 minutes) can be replaced with "반" (half) in an expression of time, much as "12:30" and "half past 12" are interchangeable. But remember not to say "반 분."

e.g. 지금 한 시 삼십 분이에요.
= 지금 한 시 반이에요.

✅QUIZ

1. Match the written times with the times shown on the clocks.

1) 여덟 시 이십 분　　2) 한 시 삼십 분　　3) 세 시 사십 분　　4) 열 시 오십오 분

a) 03:40　　b) 10:55　　c) 08:20　　d) 01:30

오전 morning, a.m.　　오후 afternoon, p.m.

17 몇 시에 일어나요?

A 몇 시에 일어나요? What time do you get up?
B 여섯 시쯤에 일어나요. I get up around 6 o'clock.

NOUN에 (시간) 3

- The particle "에" is placed after a noun of time to express when something was done or when something happened.

  e.g. A: 몇 시에 운동해요?
  B: 아홉 시에 운동해요.

➕ 쯤 Around

This word is used to express an approximate number or time.

e.g. 10시쯤에 자요.   커피를 세 잔쯤 마셔요.

###

2. Look at the schedule and mark each sentence with an "○" if true and an "×" if false.

1) 일곱 시 십 분에 일어나요. (   )
2) 세 시에 운동해요. (   )
3) 여덟 시 십 분에 학교에 가요. (   )

A 언제 아침을 먹어요? When do you eat breakfast?
B 여덟 시쯤에 아침을 먹어요. I eat breakfast around 8 o'clock.

언제 _____ 먹어요? A   B _____ 먹어요.

➕ **아침, 점심, 저녁** morning, midday, evening / breakfast, lunch, dinner

"아침," "점심," and "저녁" can express not only times of the day (morning, midday, and evening) but also the meals eaten at those times (breakfast, lunch, and dinner).

e.g. 아침 = 아침밥 / 점심 = 점심밥 / 저녁 = 저녁밥
저는 아침(밥)을 안 먹어요. / 회사에서 점심(밥)을 먹어요. / 집에서 저녁(밥)을 먹어요.

Culture

칼퇴근 When is the workday over?

The typical working hours at Korean companies are 9 am to 6 pm. Korean labor law defines the workweek as five eight-hour days (the lunch hour isn't counted as work). But anyone who has worked at a company knows that their responsibilities sometimes run past the nominal end of the workday. And in Korea in particular, workers have been traditionally worried what their boss might think if they leave the office before their boss, even if they've already finished their own work. But nowadays, young people tend to clock out as soon as the workday is over without giving their boss much thought. Going home right on the dot is called "칼퇴근" in Korea, an expression suggesting that people leave the office (퇴근) with the precision of a knife (칼). 칼퇴근 was often viewed negatively before it became an established practice, but today, people are starting to take it for granted. Do people leave the office on the dot in your home country?

언제 when   일어나다 to wake up   아침(밥) breakfast   점심(밥) lunch   저녁(밥) dinner
쯤 around (a time or number)

18 네 시부터 일곱 시까지 아르바이트를 해요

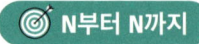 N부터 N까지

My Part-Time Work Goes from Four to Seven O'Clock

 A 오늘 수업이 있어요? Do you have class today?
B 네, 두 시부터 네 시까지 수업이 있어요. Yes, I have class from two to four o'clock.

💡 **N부터 N까지**

- "부터" expresses the starting time and "까지" expresses the ending time of some action or state. The two expressions can be used either together or separately.

  e.g. 저녁 8시**부터** 잤어요.
  도서관은 밤 열 시**까지** 문을 열어요.

- "부터" and "까지" are also used to express the starting and ending points of ranges other than time.

  e.g. 이 노래가 처음**부터** 끝**까지** 다 좋아요.
  오늘 18과**까지** 공부해요.

이 this   처음 beginning   끝 end   과 unit (in a textbook)

A 오늘 시간이 있어요? Are you free today?
B 네, 오후 다섯 시부터 시간이 있어요.
Yes, I'm free starting from 5 o'clock this afternoon.

UIZ

1. Complete each sentence based on the time shown in the picture.

1) 아침 ⇔ 밤　　　　　_____ 공부해요.
2) 1:00 ⇔ 4:00　　　　_____ 일을 해요.
3) 2:00 p.m. ⇔ 3:00 p.m.　_____ 시간이 있어요.

A 오늘 아르바이트를 해요? Do you have part-time work today?
B 네, 오후 네 시부터 일곱 시까지 아르바이트를 해요.
Yes, my part-time work goes from four to seven this afternoon.

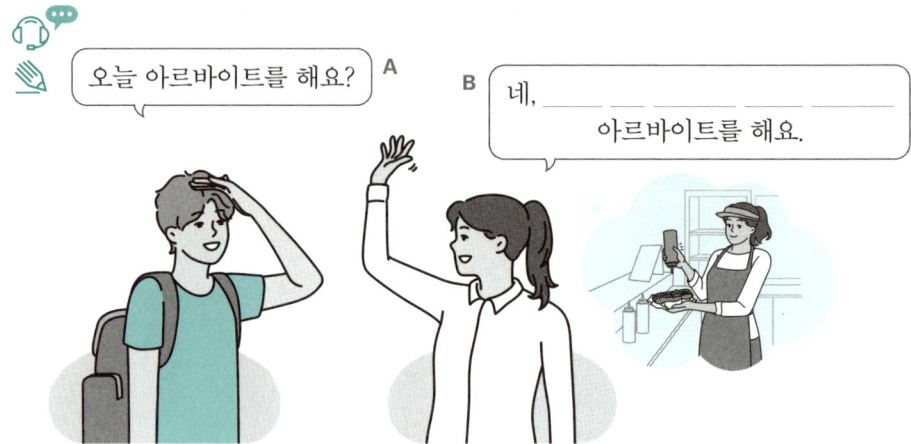

몇 시부터 몇 시까지 Asking when it starts and ends

The expressions "몇 시부터 몇 시까지" and "언제부터 언제까지" are used when asking about when something starts and when it ends.

Culture

아르바이트 Part-time job

While the Korean word "아르바이트" derives from the German word "arbeit," which means "work" in a general sense, the Korean word has the more narrow sense of a part-time job. Korean has a number of foreign loan words that are used in a different sense from the source language. For example, Koreans use the loan word "커닝" (from "cunning") to refer to peeking at prepared notes or copying another person's answers on a test, behavior that English speakers call "cheating." Koreans also say "파이팅" (from "fighting") when they want to encourage someone to stay strong amidst adversity.

아르바이트 part-time job

A 보통 몇 시부터 몇 시까지 일해요? What are your usual working hours?
B 오전 아홉 시부터 오후 다섯 시까지 일해요.
I work from nine in the morning until five in the afternoon.

 Listen to the recording and respond with your own information.

보통 몇 시부터 몇 시까지 일해요?

QUIZ

2. Complete each dialogue based on the time shown on the clocks.

1) A: 오늘 한국어 수업이 있어요?
　　B: 네, 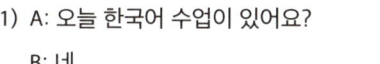 .

2) A: 몇 시부터 몇 시까지 한국어를 공부해요?
　　B: 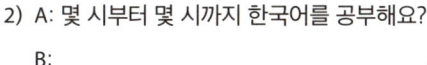 .

3) A: 언제부터 언제까지 아르바이트를 해요?
　　B: _____ .

18 네 시부터 일곱 시까지 아르바이트를 해요

19 무슨 요일에 아르바이트를 해요?
What Days of the Week Do You Work Part-Time?

A 오늘이 무슨 요일이에요? What day of the week is it today?
B 수요일이에요. It's Wednesday.

- This expression is used to ask "which" or "what" something is from a group or category of things indicated by the following noun.

  e.g. A: 무슨 음식을 먹어요?
  B: 김밥을 먹어요.

- "무슨" is also used when asking about the day of the week.

  e.g. A: 무슨 요일을 좋아해요?
  B: 토요일을 좋아해요.

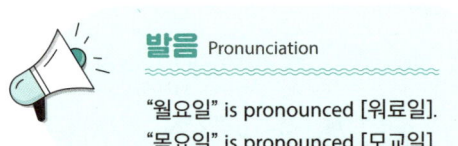

발음 Pronunciation

"월요일" is pronounced [워료일].
"목요일" is pronounced [모교일].

➕ 요일 Days of the week   = 주말

Mon.	Tue.	Wed.	Thu.	Fri.	Sat.	Sun.
월요일	화요일	수요일	목요일	금요일	토요일	일요일

무슨 which, what | 요일 day of the week | 월요일 Monday | 화요일 Tuesday | 수요일 Wednesday
목요일 Thursday | 금요일 Friday | 토요일 Saturday | 일요일 Sunday | 주말 weekend

A 무슨 요일에 아르바이트를 해요? What days of the week do you work part-time?
B 화요일하고 목요일에 해요. I work part-time on Tuesdays and Thursdays.

A _____ 아르바이트를 해요?
B _____하고 _____에 해요.

Tuesday, Thursday

QUIZ

1. Match each Korean day of the week to its English equivalent.

1) 일요일 · · Sunday
2) 화요일 · · Monday
3) 금요일 · · Tuesday
4) 토요일 · · Wednesday
5) 월요일 · · Thursday
6) 수요일 · · Friday
7) 목요일 · · Saturday

2. Answer each question based on the schedule below.

월	학교
화	친구
수	운동
목	쇼핑
금	아르바이트
토	운동
일	친구

1) A: 무슨 요일에 학교에 가요?
B: _____.

2) A: 무슨 요일에 친구를 만나요?
B: _____.

3) A: 무슨 요일에 운동해요?
B: _____.

A 무슨 아르바이트를 해요? What part-time job do you do?
B 식당에서 일해요. I work at a restaurant.

Restriction on "무슨" usage

"무슨" is used with nouns that describe things, but not nouns that describe persons.

Culture

불금 Thank God It's Friday

This is an abbreviation of "불타는 금요일," which literally means "Friday on fire." The idea is to spend one's Friday evening with the energy and excitement of a roaring fire. Young people in Korea like to say "불금" when they plan to cut loose and enjoy themselves on Friday since they have Saturday and Sunday for rest and recuperation.

A 무슨 식당에서 일해요? What restaurant do you work at?
B 중국 식당에서 일해요. I work at a Chinese restaurant.

_____에서 일해요? A

B _____에서 일해요.

QUIZ

3. Fill in the blank with the correct word.

  무슨   몇

1) A: 지금 _____ 시예요?
   B: 9시예요.

2) A: 오늘이 _____ 요일이에요?
   B: 목요일이에요.

3) A: 커피를 _____ 잔 마셔요?
   B: 두 잔 마셔요.

4) A: _____ 운동을 해요?
   B: 축구를 해요.

5) A: 사과가 _____ 개 있어요?
   B: 세 개 있어요.

4. Look at the picture and answer the question.

1) A: 무슨 과일을 좋아해요?
   B: _____.

2) A: 무슨 운동을 좋아해요?
   B: _____.

3) A: 무슨 음식을 좋아해요?
   B: _____.

4) 월 화 수 목 금 토 일
   A: 무슨 요일을 좋아해요?
   B: _____.

20 생일이 언제예요?
When Is Your Birthday?

A 오늘이 며칠이에요? What is today's date?
B 삼월 오 일이에요. It's March 5th.

Calendar Dates

- Rather than having original names for each month, Korean simply places the word "월" (month) after the appropriate Sino-Korean number ("일," "이," "삼," "사," etc.). Special attention is needed for two months with an irregular pronunciation: "6월" [유월] and "10월" [시월]. When saying the day of the month, always remember to place "일" (day) after the Sino-Korean number.

  e.g. 10월 10일 시월 십 일   6월 6일 유월 육 일

- The units of time go in order from greatest to smallest: year, month, and then day.

  e.g. 2030년 1월 1일

> ➕ _____이/가 며칠이에요? Asking about the date
>
> The expression for asking about the date is "며칠이에요?" which uses the interrogative word "며칠."
>
> e.g. 오늘이 며칠이에요?   파티가 며칠이에요?

며칠 what date   월 month   일 day   파티 party

50일 완성 한국어 1

A 삼월 십오 일에 시간이 있어요? Are you free on March 15th?
B 네, 시간이 있어요. Yes, I am.

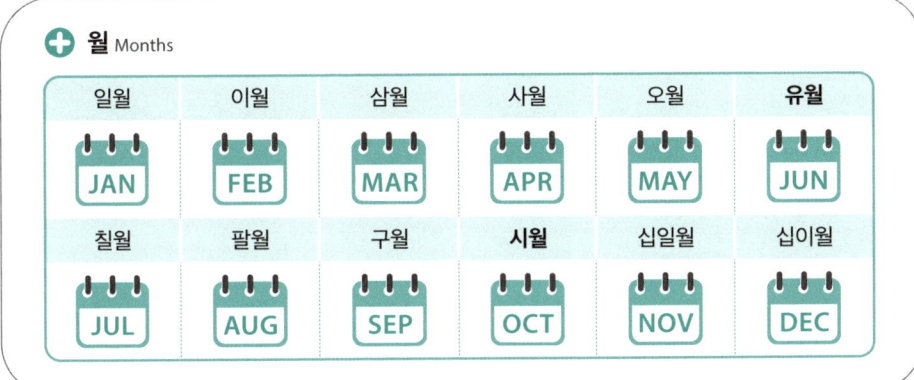

QUIZ

1. Look at each daily calendar page and write the date in hangul.

1) DEC. 8 _____

2) AUG. 7 _____

3) MAY 10 _____

4) JUN. 30 _____

A 생일이 며칠이에요? What is the date of your birthday?
B 오월 십육 일이에요. It's May 16th.

A _____이 며칠이에요?

B _____이에요.

 **발음**  Pronunciation

Special attention is needed for the pronunciation of the Sino-Korean numbers "16" [심뉵] and "26" [이심뉵].

Culture

한국의 생일 문화 Korean Birthday Culture

Koreans have a custom of eating 미역국 for breakfast on their birthday. 미역국 is a soup prepared with 미역 (sea mustard, also called wakame). It's chock-full of nutrients that thin the blood and aid in circulation, which makes it a good choice for children and nursing mothers. Traditionally, Korean mothers have eaten 미역국 and rice following childbirth. For such reasons, Koreans still like to have a bowl of 미역국 prepared for them on their birthday. When Korean young people have a birthday, their friends typically throw a party for them. Rather than a big bash, this tends to be a relaxed gathering at a restaurant or café where friends can share a meal and deliver their presents. In Korea, there's nothing wrong with sending birthday greetings before the actual day.

A 생일이 언제예요? When is your birthday?
B 십이월 팔 일이에요. It's December 8th.

A: _____이 언제예요?

B: _____ 이에요.

 Listen to the recording and respond with your own information.

생일이 언제예요?

➕ **언제예요?** When is it?

The expression "언제예요?" can also be used when asking about the date or time.

✓QUIZ

2. Check the calendar to complete each dialogue.

1) A: 오늘이 며칠이에요?
   B: _____.

2) A: 시험이 언제예요?
   B: _____.

3) A: 생일이 언제예요?
   B: _____.

시험 test

21 전화번호가 어떻게 돼요?
Can You Tell Me Your Phone Number?

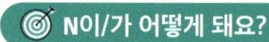 N이/가 어떻게 돼요?

 A 나이가 어떻게 돼요? Can you tell me your age?
B 저는 열아홉 살이에요. I'm 19 years old.

 N이/가 어떻게 돼요?

This expression is used to politely ask someone's phone number, name, age, job, or email address.

e.g. A: 직업이 어떻게 돼요?
B: 저는 학생이에요.

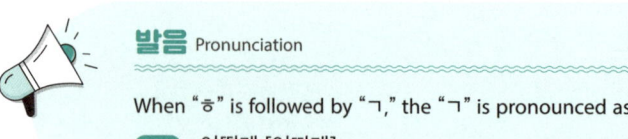

발음 Pronunciation

When "ㅎ" is followed by "ㄱ," the "ㄱ" is pronounced as [ㅋ].
e.g. 어떻게 [어떠케]

어떻게 how

A 전화번호가 어떻게 돼요? Can you tell me your phone number?
B 공일공의 일이삼사의 구칠팔사예요. It's 010-1234-9784.

A _____가 어떻게 돼요?

B _____84예요.

010-1234-9784

➕ **전화번호 읽기** Reading phone numbers

- "0" can be read either as [공] or [영], but [공] is used more often.
- The dash in the phone number is read as the possessive particle "의," but this can be pronounced [에].

e.g. 02-7900-3086 → 공이의 칠구공공의 삼공팔육
                [에]   [에]

QUIZ

1. Match the words and numerals.

1) 열여섯 살 •
                • a. 14살
                • b. 16살

2) 02-8975-6129 •
                • a. 공이-육구사오-육이삼구
                • b. 공이-팔구칠오-육일이구

2. Answer each question.

1) A: 나이가 어떻게 돼요?
   B: _____.

2) A: 전화번호가 어떻게 돼요?
   B: _____.

A 성함이 어떻게 되세요? May I ask your name?
B 저는 김미나예요. My name is Kim Mi-na.

N이/가 어떻게 되세요?

"어떻게 되세요?" ("May I ask…?") is the honorofic form of "어떻게 돼요?" ("Can you tell me…?"). It's used with people who are older or of higher social status than oneself.

e.g. 선생님, 전화번호가 어떻게 되세요?

Culture

한국식 나이 계산법 Calculating age the Korean way

The traditional way of calculating age in Korea is with a system called "세는 나이." Under that system, people are considered to be one year old at the moment of birth and get one year older at the beginning of each year, rather than on their birthday. Thus, a newborn is already one year old and will gain a year, turning two, on January 1. Some say this uniquely Korean method of calculating age reflects a profound respect for the sanctity of life, treating the fetus in the womb as a living creature. In contrast, the international standard for calculating age (called "만 나이") starts at 0 at the date of birth and goes up one year with each birthday. In regard to the two systems, many Koreans support the idea of fully adopting "만 나이." Compared to "세는 나이," that would have the effect of shaving two years off the age of Koreans who haven't had their birthday yet that year. Which system sounds better to you?

성함 name (honorific)

A 연세가 어떻게 되세요? May I ask your age?
B 쉰한 살이에요. I'm 51 years old.

┌─ ➕ 제목 ──┐
│ 나이 age, plain < 연세 age, honorific   │ 이름 name, plain < 성함 name, honorific │
│   │
│ The honorific form of "나이" is "연세," and the honorific form of "이름" is "성함." │
│   │
│ e.g. 나이가 몇 살이에요? → 연세가 어떻게 되세요?   │
│   이름이 뭐예요? → 성함이 어떻게 되세요?   │
└──┘

QUIZ

3. Match each question with the appropriate answer.

1) 연세가 어떻게 되세요?   •   • a) 저는 히로 마사오예요.
2) 성함이 어떻게 되세요?   •   • b) 010-3789-49967이에요.
3) 직업이 어떻게 되세요?   •   • c) 저는 쉰 살이에요.
4) 전화번호가 어떻게 되세요?   •   • d) 저는 선생님이에요.

연세 age (honorific)   쉰 fifty (pure Korean number)

22. 은행이 어디에 있어요?
Where Is the Bank?

 N이/가 N에 있다

A 은행이 어디에 있어요? Where is the bank?
B 일 층에 있어요. It's on the first floor.

N이/가 N에 있다/없다

- In addition to its sense of possession, "있다" can also be used to express the existence or location of a person or thing, with the particle "에" attached to the noun of location. When you want to say that a person or thing is not at a given location, the verb "없다" is used instead of "있다."

  e.g. 다니엘이 도서관에 있어요.
  다니엘이 집에 없어요.

- The order of the subject (N이/가) and the noun of location (N에) can be reversed.

  e.g. 다니엘이 집에 있어요. = 집에 다니엘이 있어요.

은행 bank   층 floor

A 은행이 일 층에 있어요? Is the bank on the first floor?
B 아니요, 일 층에 없어요. 이 층에 있어요. No, it's not. It's on the second floor.

은행이 ___ ___ 있어요? A

B 아니요, ___ ___ 없어요. ___ ___ 있어요.

➕ 몇 층에 있어요? What floor is it?

When talking about the floor of a building, the Sino-Korean numbers "일," "이," "삼," "사," etc. are attached after the noun "층" (floor). When asking which floor a person or thing is on, you can say "몇 층에 있어요?" in addition to the more generic "어디에 있어요?"

3 삼 층
2 이 층
1 일 층

Culture

4층 Superstition about the number 4 in Korea

In Korea and other countries influenced by the Chinese language, there's a tendency to avoid the number four ("사") because it's pronounced the same as the Chinese character for death (死, "사"). Elevators installed in Korean buildings sometimes list "F" in place of "4" for the fourth floor. For the same reason, Incheon International Airport skips Nos. 4 and 44 in the sequence of boarding gates.

QUIZ

1. Look at the floor chart and complete each sentence.

3 Floor 미용실
2 Floor 은행
1 Floor 카페

1) 미용실이 _____.
2) 은행이 _____.
3) 카페가 _____.

미용실 hair salon

A 화장실이 어디에 있어요? Where is the restroom?
B 은행 옆에 있어요. It's next to the bank.

N이/가 N 위/아래/앞/etc.에 있다

"에 있다" is often used alongside nouns of position such as "위," "아래," "앞," etc. in order to specify the location of a person or thing. Pay special attention to the word order used in such cases.

e.g. 우유가 책상 위에 있어요 (O)   위에 책상 (X)   위 책상에 (X)

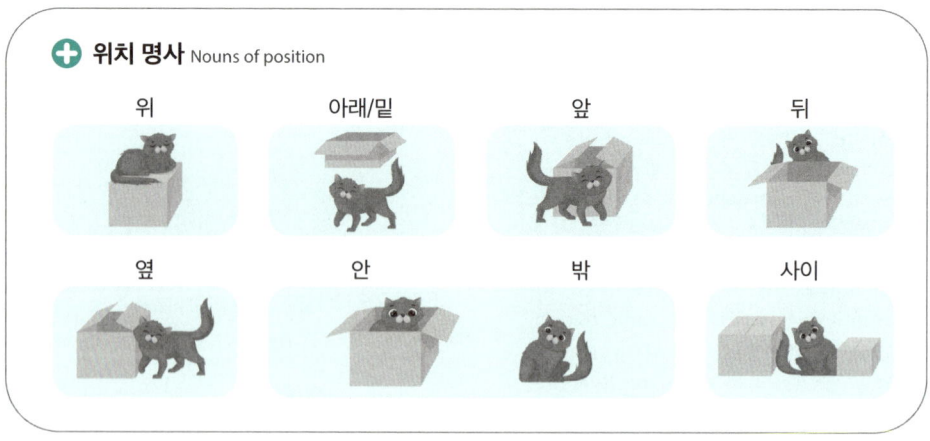

위 above   아래/밑 below   앞 in front of   뒤 behind   옆 beside   안 inside   밖 outside
사이 between

A 에이티엠(ATM)이 어디에 있어요? Where is the ATM?
B 은행 밖에 있어요. It's outside the bank.

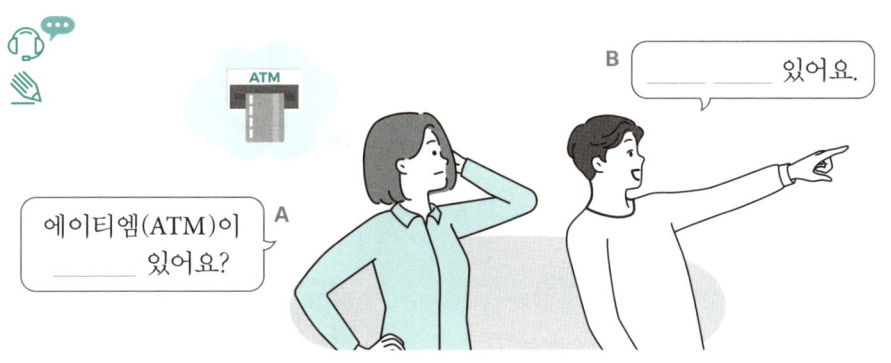

Listen to the recording and respond with your own information.

화장실이 어디에 있어요?

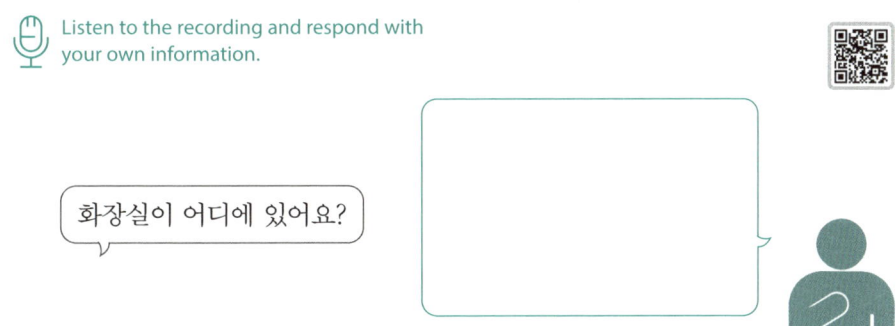

QUIZ

2. Look at the floor chart and complete each sentence.

1) A: 약국이 어디에 있어요?
   B: 병원 _____.

2) A: 병원 위에 뭐가 있어요?
   B: _____.

3) A: 카페가 어디에 있어요?
   B: 병원 _____.

3 Floor	미용실		화장실
2 Floor	병원		약국
1 Floor	카페		

에이티엠 ATM

23 아래층으로 가세요
Go Downstairs

A 화장실이 어디에 있어요? Where is the restroom?
B 아래층으로 가세요. Go downstairs.

This particle is used with verbs of movement to express the direction of movement. "로" is used when the preceding noun has no batchim or has the batchim "ㄹ," and "으로" is used when the noun has a batchim other than "ㄹ."

받침 X	+ 로	아래 → 아래로
받침 ㄹ		서울 → 서울로
받침 O	+ 으로	집 → 집으로

e.g. A: 식당이 어디에 있어요?
B: 1층으로 가세요.

화장실 restroom

A 구두가 어디에 있어요? Where are the dress shoes?
B 위층으로 가세요. Go upstairs.

➕ N에 vs. N(으)로

- When the particle "에" is used with a verb of movement, the noun in front of "에" indicates the destination.

  e.g. 학교에 가요.

- When the particle "(으)로" is used with a verb of movement, the noun in front of "(으)로" indicates the direction of movement or the route to the destination.

  e.g. 학교로 가요.

- That said, the two particles often mean roughly the same thing when used with verbs of movement.

  e.g. A: 어디에 가요?   =   A: 어디로 가요?
       B: 집에 가요.   B: 집으로 가요.

 QUIZ

1. Choose the correct form of the particle "(으)로."

1) 저는 식당(로, 으로) 가요.

2) A: 지금 어디(로, 으로) 가요?
   B: 학교(로, 으로) 가요.

3) A: 과일이 어디에 있어요?
   B: 3층(로, 으로) 가세요.

4) 마이클 씨는 여기(로, 으로) 오세요.

A 이 버스는 어디로 가요? Where is this bus going?
B 서울로 가요. It's going to Seoul.

➕ 앞, 뒤, 옆, 위, 아래, 오른쪽, 왼쪽 + (으)로

When a noun of position ("앞," "뒤," "옆," "위," "아래," etc.) is used with a noun of location and followed by a verb of movement, the particle "(으)로" is used rather than "에."

e. g. A: 화장실이 어디에 있어요?
B: 오른쪽으로 가세요. (O)   오른쪽에 가세요. (✗)

 QUIZ

2. Choose the correct form of the particle "(으)로."

1) A: 여행 가요?
   B: 네, 독일(로, 으로) 가요.
2) A: 이 버스는 어디로 가요?
   B: 경주(로, 으로) 가요.
3) A: 어디에 가요?
   B: 시장(로, 으로) 가요.
4) A: 여러분, 교실(로, 으로) 오세요.
   B: 네, 선생님.

3. Fill in the blanks with the correct particles.

에 / (으)로 / 에서

1) 화장실은 아래층(   ) 있어요.
2) 백화점(   ) 옷을 사요.
3) 1층(   ) 구두가 있어요.
4) 앞(   ) 오세요.
5) 지하철역이 오른쪽(   ) 있어요.
   오른쪽(   ) 가세요.

버스 bus   여행 trip   교실 classroom   백화점 department store   오른쪽 the right side
왼쪽 the left side

A 백화점이 어디에 있어요? Where is the department store?
B 앞으로 쭉 가세요. Go straight ahead.

_____ 어디에 있어요? A
B _____ 쭉 가세요.

Culture

신호등 색깔 When the traffic signal turns blue

Traffic signals come in three colors — red, yellow, and green — but Koreans refer to the green light (초록불) as the "blue" light (파란불). That might leave foreigners wondering about the whereabouts of the elusive blue light. So why is the green light called the blue light in Korean? A long time ago, Koreans thought that red, blue, white, black, and yellow were the five basic colors. Back then, they didn't distinguish green from blue but just referred to them both as blue. That's why the green traffic light is still called the blue light today. Grass can also be described as "blue" in Korean. So what color traffic light should you wait for before crossing the street in Korea? Try answering the question in Korean!

쭉 straight (ahead)

24 어제 집에서 쉬었어요
I Rested at Home Yesterday

🎯 A/V-았어요/었어요

A 어제 도서관에 갔어요? Did you go to the library yesterday?
B 네, 도서관에 갔어요. Yes, I did.

💡 A/V-았어요/었어요 1

This grammar construction is used with verbs or adjectives to express a past action or state. When the verb or adjective's final vowel is "ㅏ, ㅗ," "-았어요" is placed at the end. When the verb or adjective ends in "-하다," "-했어요" is placed at the end.

ㅏ, ㅗ + 았어요		
받다 + -았어요	→	받았어요
사다 + -았어요	→	샀어요
보다 + -았어요	→	봤어요

-하다 → 했어요		
일하다		일했어요
공부하다	→	공부했어요
이야기하다		이야기했어요

A 어제 뭐 했어요? What did you do yesterday?
B 도서관에서 공부했어요. I studied at the library.

A: 어제 _____ ?
B: 도서관에서 _____ .

Culture

한국의 등산 문화 Korean hiking culture

About 70% of Korean territory is mountainous, and there are over 4,000 mountains in the country. No wonder hiking is such a popular outdoor activity there! Interestingly, Koreans pull out their finest hiking outfits and fanciest equipment, such as trekking poles, just for a modest hike near their house. So if you happen to walk down a trail in a Korean neighborhood, you're likely to spot fellow hikers decked out in professional-quality hiking attire in eye-popping hues of red and orange.

QUIZ

1. Choose the correct conjugation of the verb.

1) 저는 어제 학교에 (가요 / 갔어요).
2) 지금 뭐 (먹어요 / 먹었어요)?
3) 지금 아르바이트를 (해요 / 했어요).
4) 그저께 친구를 (만나요 / 만났어요)?
5) 어제 오후에 영화를 (봐요 / 봤어요).
6) 저는 보통 아침 7시에 (일어나요 / 일어났어요).

A 어제 뭐 했어요? What did you do yesterday?
B 집에서 쉬었어요. 유나 씨는요? I rested at home. What about you, Yu-na?
A 책을 읽었어요. I read a book.

____ 뭐 했어요? A

B 집에서 ____.
유나 씨 ____?

책을 읽었어요. A

💡 A/V-았어요/었어요 2

This grammar construction is used with verbs or adjectives to express a past action or state. When the verb or adjective's final vowel is not "ㅏ, ㅗ" and when it does not end in "-하다," "-었어요" is placed at the end.

in all other cases + -었어요		
먹다 + -었어요	→	먹었어요
읽다 + -었어요	→	읽었어요
마시다 + -었어요	→	마셨어요
쉬다 + -었어요	→	쉬었어요

➕ _ 씨는요? What about you?

It's common in conversation to turn a question around and ask the other person's opinion about it. In Korea, there's no need to repeat the question in full: simply say the other person's name followed by "은/는요?"

A 주말에 뭐 했어요? What did you over the weekend?
B 책을 많이 읽었어요. 책이 아주 재미있었어요.
I read a lot of books. The books were very interesting.

Listen to the recording and respond with your own information.

주말에 뭐 했어요?

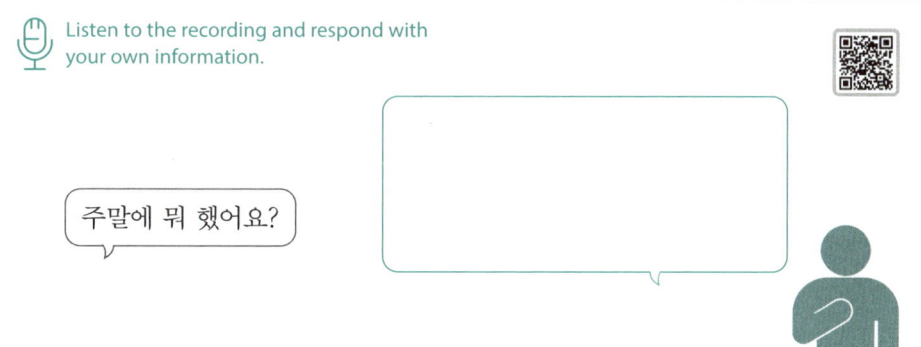

QUIZ

2. Choose the right words and conjugate them correctly to complete the paragraph below.

가다 / 마시다 / 만나다 / 먹다 / 보다 / 샤워하다 / 재미있다 / 하다

저는 어제 일찍 일어났어요. 먼저 밥을 1) _____. 그리고 2) _____.
오후에 시내에서 친구를 3) _____. 우리는 영화관에 4) _____.
같이 영화를 5) _____. 그리고 카페에서 차를 6) _____. 그리고
이야기를 많이 7) _____. 정말 8) _____.

주말 weekend   많이 many, a lot   먼저 first, ahead

25 책을 읽고 잤어요
I Read a Book and Went to Bed

 V-고

A 일요일에 뭐 해요? What do you do on Sundays?
B 운동하고 쉬어요. I exercise and rest.

 V-고

- This grammar construction is used with verbs when listing two things chronologically (in the order that they occurred).

받침 X	+ 고	보고
받침 O		먹고

- The subject of the first and second clause must be the same in this construction, and the subject is omitted from the second clause.
  - e.g. 저는 밥을 먹어요. + 저는 커피를 마셔요. → 저는 밥을 먹고 커피를 마셔요.

- Reversing the order of the clauses changes their meaning.
  - e.g. 저는 밥을 먹고 커피를 마셔요. ≠ 저는 커피를 마시고 밥을 먹어요.

- When talking about past occurrences, the past tense is only used in the final verb and not in the verb before "-고."
  - e.g. 저는 어제 밥을 먹었어요. + 저는 커피를 마셨어요.
    → 저는 어제 밥을 먹었고 커피를 마셨어요. (✕)
    → 저는 어제 밥을 먹고 커피를 마셨어요. (O)

A 어제 뭐 했어요? What did you do yesterday?
B 책을 읽고 잤어요. I read a book and went to bed.

➕ 그리고 and

A compound sentence with two clauses connected by "-고" can be divided into two sentences by replacing "-고" with "그리고."

e.g. 저는 밥을 먹고 커피를 마셔요.
→ 저는 밥을 먹어요. 그리고 커피를 마셔요.

저는 어제 밥을 먹고 커피를 마셨어요.
→ 저는 어제 밥을 먹었어요. 그리고 커피를 마셨어요.

➕ -고 and

"-고" can be used to connect more than two sentences.

e.g. 저는 공부했어요. + 밥을 먹었어요. + 잤어요.
→ 저는 공부하고 밥을 먹고 잤어요.

✅ QUIZ

1. Connect the sentences using "-고."

1) 한국어를 배워요. + 친구를 만나요. ➡ 한국어를 (　　　) 친구를 만나요.
2) 운동을 해요. + 물을 마셔요. ➡ 운동을 (　　　) 물을 마셔요.
3) 영화를 봤어요. + 집에 갔어요. ➡ 영화를 (　　　) 집에 갔어요.
4) 숙제를 했어요. + 쉬었어요. ➡ 숙제를 (　　　) 쉬었어요.

A 지금 뭐 먹어요? What are you eating right now?
B 저는 김밥을 먹고 친구는 냉면을 먹어요.
I'm eating gimbap, and my friend is eating naengmyeon.

 A/V-고

- "-고" can also be used to list two separate facts rather than listing two things in chronological order. This grammar construction can be used with both verbs and adjectives.

    e.g. 마이클 씨는 한국어를 배우고 영어를 가르쳐요.
    냉면이 시원하고 맛있어요.

- This construction can be used even when the subjects of the first and second clause are different. Reversing the order of the clauses does not change their meaning.

    e.g. 저는 책을 읽고 친구는 운동해요. = 친구는 운동하고 저는 책을 읽어요.

 발음 Pronunciation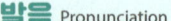

- The double batchim "ㄺ" is pronounced as [ㄱ] at the end of a word or before a consonant.
- One exception is "읽," which is pronounced [일] (not [익]) when it comes before "ㄱ."

    e.g. 읽고 [일꼬]

A 김밥이 맛있어요? Does gimbap taste good?
B 네, 싸고 맛있어요. Yes, it's cheap and tastes good.

A 김밥이 _____ ?
B 네, _____ 맛있어요.

Culture

광장시장 Gwangjang Market

Gwangjang Market, located in Seoul's Jongno District, is Korea's largest traditional market. There's a famous 먹거리 골목 (food alley) in the market lined with restaurants selling 빈대떡, 김밥, 잔치국수, 육회, and 찹쌀꽈배기, so the area draws tourists not only on weekends but also during the week. Koreans are fond of eating the savory pancakes known as 빈대떡 on rainy days. According to a survey conducted by an e-commerce company, sales of 부침개 (a culinary category including 빈대떡 and similar dishes) were 169% higher when it rained than when it did not. So the next time it rains, how about dropping by Gwangjang Market to sample some of its famously delicious 빈대떡?

QUIZ

2. Connect the sentences using "-고" or "하고."

-고   하고

1) 저는 학교에 가요. + 친구는 공원에 가요. ➡ 저는 학교에 (　　　) 친구는 공원에 가요.
2) 저는 사과를 사요. + 주스를 사요. ➡ 저는 사과(　　　) 주스를 사요.
3) 김밥이 싸요. + 김밥이 맛있어요. ➡ 김밥이 (　　　) 맛있어요.
4) 책이 있어요. + 연필이 있어요. ➡ 책(　　　) 연필이 있어요.
5) 알리사 씨는 독일어를 가르쳐요. + 한국어를 배워요.
   ➡ 알리사 씨는 독일어를 (　　　) 한국어를 배워요.

26 순두부찌개가 맵지만 맛있어요   A/V-지만

Sundubu-jjigae Is Spicy, but It Tastes Good

A 순두부찌개가 어때요? How is sundubu-jjigae?
B 맵지만 맛있어요. It's spicy, but it tastes good.

A 순두부찌개___ 어때요?
B ___ 맛있어요.

A/V-지만 1

This is used to express two opposing facts or situations.

받침 X	+ 지만	비싸**지만** 맛있어요
받침 O		맛있**지만** 비싸요

➕ __이/가 어때요? How is it?

This is used when asking another person "how" something is.

e.g. 김치가 어때요?
그 책이 어때요?

맵다 to be spicy   그 that

A 집이 어때요? How is your house?
B 좀 멀지만 좋아요. It's a little far, but it's nice.

Listen to the recording and respond with your own information.

집이 어때요?

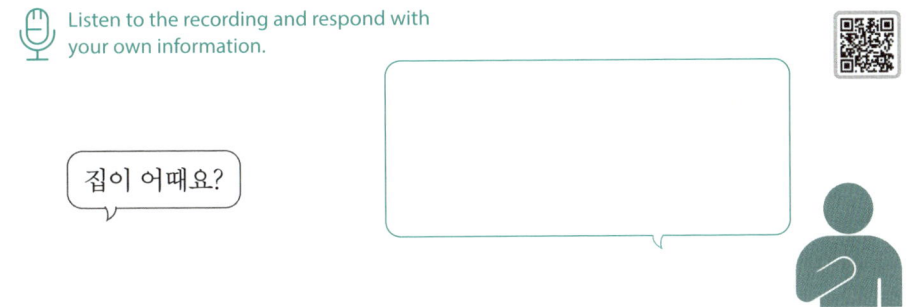

QUIZ

1. Complete the sentence using the words.

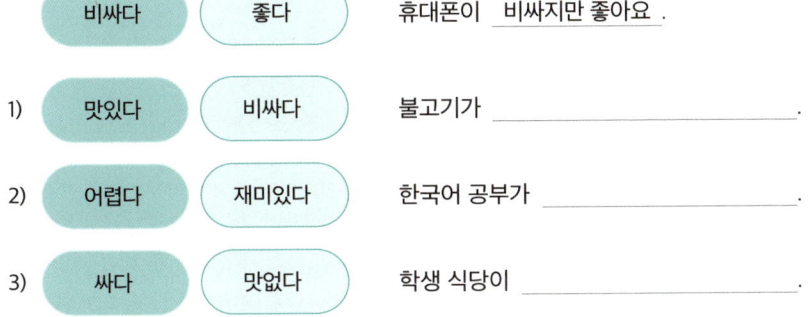

| 비싸다 | 좋다 | 휴대폰이 <u>비싸지만 좋아요</u>. |

1) 맛있다 / 비싸다 — 불고기가 _____.
2) 어렵다 / 재미있다 — 한국어 공부가 _____.
3) 싸다 / 맛없다 — 학생 식당이 _____.

멀다 to be far   어렵다 to be difficult   학생 식당 school cafeteria

A 고기를 먹어요? Do you eat meat?
B 아니요, 생선은 먹지만 고기는 안 먹어요. No. I eat fish, but I don't eat meat.

A/V-지만 2

- "은/는" is often placed after the subjects or objects of two sentences connected with "지만" to draw a contrast between time and other matters.

  e.g. 저는 고기를 먹지만 다니엘은 고기를 안 먹어요.
  저는 고기는 먹지만 생선은 안 먹어요.
  저는 지금은 고기를 먹지만 전에는 고기를 안 먹었어요.

- The first clause connected with "지만" can be conjugated in the past tense with "-았/었지만"

  e.g. 많이 공부했지만 시험을 잘 못 봤어요.

Culture

안 매운 김치도 있어요 Not all kinds of kimchi are spicy

Kimchi is one of the best-known Korean dishes that's prepared by soaking vegetables (such as Napa cabbage, radishes, or cucumbers) in a salt brine, covering them in seasoning, and then letting them ferment. There's quite a range of kimchi types, with many regional variations. Kimchi tends to be spicy in the southwestern Honam (Jeolla) region and salty in the southeastern Yeongnam (Gyeongsang) region. The cold regions in the north are best-known for kimchi types with little or no chili pepper powder, such as baek-kimchi, bossam-kimchi, and dongchimi. If you find kimchi too spicy for your taste, we encourage you to try baek-kimchi or dongchimi.

생선 (cooked) fish   자주 often   시험을 잘 못 보다 to do poorly on a test

A 쇼핑을 자주 해요? Do you often go shopping?
B 아니요, 전에는 쇼핑을 자주 했지만 요즘에는 자주 안 해요.
No. I often went shopping in the past, but I don't nowadays.

쇼핑을 자주 해요? A

B 아니요, 전에는 쇼핑을 자주 _____
   요즘에는 _____.

QUIZ

2. Complete each sentence as shown in the example.

불고기	냉면
비싸요.	안 비싸요.

➡ 불고기는 비싸지만 냉면은 안 비싸요 .

1)
저	친구
김치를 좋아해요.	김치를 안 먹어요.

➡ _____.

2)
어제	오늘
도서관에 갔어요.	집에서 쉬어요.

➡ _____.

3)
전에	지금
김치를 안 먹었어요.	김치를 먹어요.

➡ _____.

전 in the past   요즘 nowadays

27 유튜브를 보거나 책을 읽어요
I Watch YouTube or Read a Book

A 저녁에 보통 뭐 해요? What do you usually do in the evening?
B 유튜브를 보거나 책을 읽어요. I watch YouTube or read a book.

A ___ 보통 뭐 해요?
B 유튜브를 ___ 책을 읽어요.

V-거나

- This grammar construction expresses a choice between several facts (or actions).

받침 X	+ 거나	보거나
받침 O		듣거나

e.g. 음악을 듣거나 텔레비전을 봐요.

- "-거나" can be used to connect two or more verb phrases.

e.g. A: 주말에 뭐 해요?
B: 집에서 쉬거나 유튜브를 보거나 청소해요.

A 요즘 무슨 운동을 해요? What exercise do you do these days?
B 공원에서 걷거나 자전거를 타요. I walk in the park or ride a bike.

QUIZ

1. Look at the picture and fill in the blanks with the correct verb forms.

1) A: 아침에 뭘 먹어요?
   B: 밥을 _____ 우유를 _____.

2) A: 일요일에 뭐 해요?
   B: 산에 _____ 공원에서 _____.

3) A: 백화점에서 뭐 해요?
   B: 옷을 _____ 친구를 _____.

A 편의점에서 뭘 해요? What do you do at a convenience store?
B 라면을 먹거나 물건을 사요. I eat ramen noodles or buy items.

A _____ 뭘 해요?

B 라면을 _____ 물건을 _____.

Culture

한국의 편의점 Korean convenience stores

Korea has a huge number of convenience stores, and they're generally open 24-7. While convenience stores obviously sell a wide range of items, shopping is just one of many things you can do there. Koreans like to stop by for a quick meal of ramen noodles, gimbap, or 도시락 (lunchbox-style food). The stores have a hot water dispenser for your instant noodles, as well as a microwave for warming up your 도시락. You can even drop off packages there for a courier to pick up or handle your electricity or water bill. You might be surprised to find music CDs for sale, along with tickets for concerts and sporting events like basketball or soccer games. The stores are stocked with undergarments, socks, and toiletries, and you can even buy lottery tickets there. Be sure to check out a convenience store while you're in Korea!

편의점 convenience store   물건 thing, item

A 카페에서 뭘 해요? What do you do at a cafe?
B 음악을 듣거나 책을 읽어요. I listen to music or read a book.

QUIZ

2. Look at the pictures below and talk about what you usually do on the weekend.

저는 주말에 청소하거나 운동해요.

| 공부 | 친구 | 요리 | 자전거 | 쇼핑 | 김밥 |
| 커피 | 잠 | 텔레비전 | 컴퓨터 | 등산 | 술 |

27 유튜브를 보거나 책을 읽어요

28 빨래나 청소를 해요
I Do the Laundry or the Cleaning

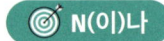

A 아침에 보통 뭘 먹어요? What do you usually eat for breakfast?
B 샌드위치나 김밥을 먹어요. I eat a sandwich or gimbap.

아침에 보통 뭘 _____? **A**
B 샌드위치___ 김밥_____.

N(이)나

This grammar construction is placed after a noun to indicate that a choice is made between what comes before and what comes after.

받침 X	+ 나	샌드위치**나** 김밥
받침 O	+ 이나	김밥**이나** 샌드위치

샌드위치 sandwich

A 아침에 보통 뭘 먹어요? What do you usually eat for breakfast?
B 김밥이나 샌드위치를 먹어요. I eat gimbap or a sandwich.

아침에 보통 뭘 _____? A

B 김밥___ 샌드위치___ _____.

 Listen to the recording and respond with your own information.

점심에 보통 뭘 먹어요?

QUIZ

1. Fill in the blank with "이나" or "나."

1)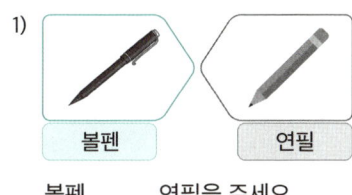
볼펜_____ 연필을 주세요.

2)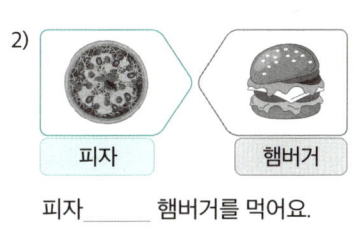
피자_____ 햄버거를 먹어요.

3)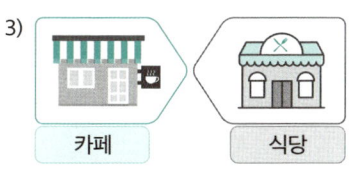
카페_____ 식당에 가요.

4)
도서관_____ 집에서 공부해요.

28 빨래나 청소를 해요 123

A 주말에 보통 뭘 해요? What do you usually do on the weekend?
B 빨래나 청소나 요리를 해요. I do the laundry, the cleaning, or the cooking.

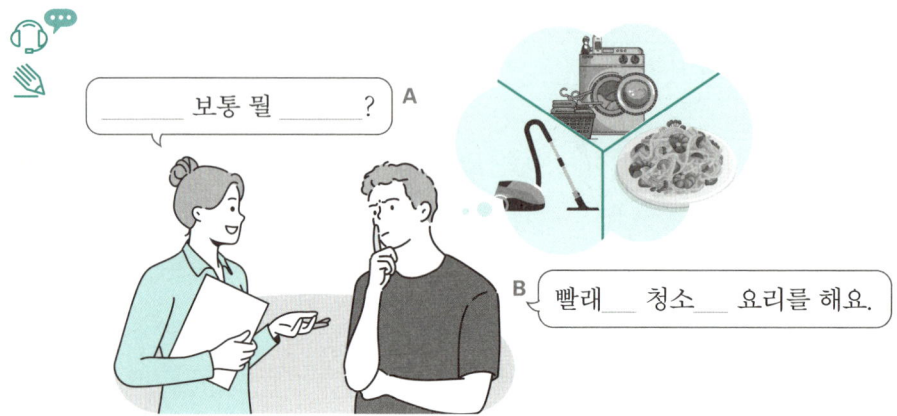

A: 보통 뭘 _____?
B: 빨래___ 청소___ 요리를 해요.

(이)나 vs. -거나

Considering that "(이)나" indicates a choice between several options, the verb that comes after "(이)나" needs to be compatible with all the nouns listed before it. When the nouns in question take different verbs, you should use the "-거나" grammar construction instead.

e.g. 드라마나 영화를 봐요. (O)
텔레비전이나 인터넷을 해요. (X) → 텔레비전을 보거나 인터넷을 해요. (O)

Culture

술 마신 다음 날 아침에는 해장국 Haejangguk for breakfast after a night of drinking

Haejangguk is a soup that's eaten to ease an upset stomach the morning after a drinking party. Koreans will spoon up rice dunked in the hot broth to help them get over their hangover. Each region has its own unique spin on haejangguk. Some of the most famous ingredients added to the soup are coagulated cow blood in the Cheongjin-dong neighborhood of Seoul, dried pollack in Mugyo-dong, pork bones in Yangpyeong, and soybean sprouts in Jeonju. Are there any special foods in your country that are eaten after a bender?

인터넷을 하다 to use the internet

A 보통 어디에서 친구를 만나요? Where do you usually meet your friends?
B 식당이나 카페나 영화관에서 만나요.
We meet at a restaurant, a cafe, or a movie theater.

보통 어디에서 친구를 만나요? A

식당___ 카페___ 영화관에서 만나요. B

 Listen to the recording and respond with your own information.

주말에 보통 뭘 해요?

QUIZ

2. Complete each dialogue using "(이)나."

1) 수영   태권도
A: 무슨 운동을 자주 해요?
B: _____.

2) 파스타   샐러드   피자
A: 무슨 음식을 자주 만들어요?
B: _____.

3) 금요일   토요일
A: 보통 무슨 요일에 친구를 만나요?
B: _____.

음식을 만들다 to make food   파스타 pasta   샐러드 salad   피자 pizza

29 방학에 고향에 갈 거예요
I'm Going to Go to My Hometown for the Vacation

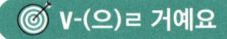

A 방학에 뭐 할 거예요? What are you going to do during the vacation?
B 고향에 갈 거예요. I'm going to go to my hometown.

방학에 뭐 _____ ? A

B 고향에 _____.

V-(으)ㄹ 거예요

This combines with the verb to describe a future situation.

받침 X	+ -ㄹ 거예요	보다 → 볼 거예요
받침 ㄹ		만들다 → 만들 거예요
받침 O	+ -을 거예요	먹다 → 먹을 거예요

e.g. A: 주말에 뭐 할 거예요?
B: 친구를 만날 거예요.

발음 Pronunciation

The "ㄱ" that comes after "-(으)ㄹ" is pronounced as [ㄲ].

e.g. 갈 거예요 [갈 꺼예요]
먹을 거예요 [머글 꺼예요]

방학 (school) vacation   고향 hometown   만들다 to make

A 점심에 뭐 먹을 거예요? What are you going to eat for lunch?
B 비빔밥을 먹을 거예요. I'm going to eat bibimbap.

QUIZ

1. Look at the weekly calendar and choose the correct verb form.

1) 저는 월요일에 　　　　공부했어요. ☐ 　　공부할 거예요. ☐
2) 저는 금요일에 친구를 　만났어요. ☐ 　　만날 거예요. ☐
3) 저는 수요일에 　　　　운동했어요. ☐ 　　운동할 거예요. ☐
4) 저는 토요일에 산에 　　갔어요. ☐ 　　갈 거예요. ☐

A 주말에 뭐 할 거예요? What are you going to do on the weekened?
B 아침에 운동하고 집에서 쉴 거예요.
I'm going to exercise in the morning and then relax at home.

A 주말에 뭐 _____?

B 아침에 _____ 집에서 _____.

➕ Connecting sentences in the future tense

The future tense is not used before "-고" even when talking about something that will happen in the future. The tense is marked in the following verb.

e.g. 주말에 친구를 만날 거예요. + 한국어를 공부할 거예요.
→ 주말에 친구를 만나고 한국어를 공부할 거예요.

Culture

한국의 방학 Korean school vacations

Students get vacations at Korean schools. Summer vacation typically runs for a little under a month, from July 17 to August 15. Winter vacation is longer than summer vacation, going from late December to late January or early February. Korean students are given homework assignments to do over the vacation. All students' classes are generally over in February, and the new semester doesn't start until March. But since graduation and closing ceremony are held in February, students still have to go back to school after winter vacation. With the regular course of study already completed, students are often encouraged to study on their own during that time. Many schools also have a short spring break, lasting ten days or so, until the new semester begins in March. There's no homework over spring break, however. Do students have to do homework over school vacation in your home country?

A 내일 뭐 해요? What are you doing tomorrow?
B 저는 내일 친구를 만나요. I'm meeting my friends tomorrow.

A: 내일 뭐 _____ ?
B: 저는 내일 친구를 _____ .

➕ The near future

The present tense ending "-아요/어요" can be used instead of "-(으)ㄹ 거예요" for things that are happening in the near future.

e.g. A: 내일 운동해요?
　　　B: 아니요, 내일 운동 안 해요.

✅ QUIZ

2. Complete the sentence using "-(으)ㄹ 거예요" and answer the question.

1) A: 내일 친구를 _____ ? (만나다)
　　B: _____ .

2) A: 내일 _____ ? (운동하다)
　　B: _____ .

3) A: 내일 백화점에서 뭐 _____ ? (사다)
　　B: _____ .

4) A: 내일 무슨 음식을 _____ ? (먹다)
　　B: _____ .

5) A: 내일 누구를 _____ ? (만나다)
　　B: _____ .

30 그냥 집에서 쉬려고 해요
I'm Just Planning to Relax at Home

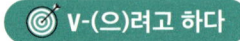 V-(으)려고 하다

 A 주말에 뭐 할 거예요? What are you going to do on the weekend?
B 그냥 집에서 쉬려고 해요. I'm just planning to relax at home.

V-(으)려고 하다

- This grammar structure is used to indicate the subject's intention or plan to do something.

받침 X	+ -려고 하다	사려고 하다
받침 ㄹ		만들려고 하다
받침 O	+ -으려고 하다	읽으려고 하다
		먹으려고 하다

- In colloquial speech, this is often used in the form "-(으)려고요."

  e.g. A: 주말에 뭐 할 거예요?
  B: 집에서 쉬려고요.

그냥 just, only

A 유나 씨는 주말에 뭘 하려고 해요?
What are you planning to do on the weekend, Yu-na?
B 저는 책을 읽으려고 해요. I'm planning to read a book.

유나 씨는 주말에 뭘 하려고 해요? A

B 저는 책을 _____.

 Listen to the recording and respond with your own information.

주말에 뭐 할 거예요?

QUIZ

1. Look at the picture and complete the sentence with "-(으)려고 하다."

1)
주말에 백화점에서 쇼핑을 _____.

2)
오늘 저녁에 시내에서 친구를 _____.

3)
토요일에 집을 _____.

4)
주말에 공원에서 사진을 _____.

사진을 찍다 to take a photograph

30 그냥 집에서 쉬려고 해요

A 그 영화를 봤어요? Have you seen that movie?
B 아니요. 아직 안 봤어요. 오늘 밤에 보려고 해요.
No, I haven't seen it yet. I'm planning to see it tonight.

V-(으)려고 하다

"-(으)려고 했다" is used to indicate that the subject had intended to do something in the past.

e.g. 작년에 프랑스에 여행을 **가려고 했어요**. 그런데 비행기표가 너무 비쌌어요. 그래서 안 갔어요.

Culture

한국의 학제 Korean education system

Korean education currently consists of six years in elementary school, three years in middle school, three years in high school, and four years in university. The nine years of elementary and middle school, which are compulsory, are provided for free. High school education is also free, though not compulsory. Since Koreans tend to take education very seriously, almost all students make it into high school and 67% are admitted to university. This system of education has been retained since 1951. Is your country's education system similar to or different from Korea's?

A 어제 영화를 봤어요? Did you see that movie yesterday?

B 아니요, 보려고 했어요. 그런데 너무 피곤했어요. 그래서 그냥 잤어요.
No, I was planning to see it. But I was too tired, so I just fell asleep.

A: 그 영화를 봤어요?

B: 아니요, _____.
그런데 너무 피곤했어요.
그래서 그냥 잤어요.

QUIZ

2. Look at the picture and complete the sentence.

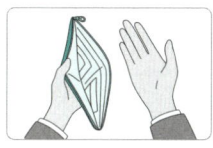
1) A: 어제 책을 샀어요?
   B: 아니요, 책을 _____. 그런데 돈이 없었어요.

2) A: 어제 숙제를 했어요?
   B: 아니요, 숙제를 _____. 그런데 너무 피곤했어요.
   그래서 잤어요.

3) A: 왜 오늘 병원에 안 갔어요?
   B: 병원에 _____. 그런데 시간이 없었어요.

4) A: 왜 전화를 안 했어요?
   B: 전화를 _____. 그런데 배터리가 없었어요.

아직 still, yet   피곤하다 to be tired   왜 why   배터리 battery

31 기차로 부산에 갈 거예요
I'm Going to Go to Busan by Train

 N(으)로 (2)

A 부산에 어떻게 갈 거예요? How are you going to go to Busan?
B 기차로 갈 거예요. I'm going to go on the train.

 N-(으)로 2

"(으)로" indicates the means, method, or tool used to do something.

받침 X	+ 로	버스 → 버스로
받침 ㄹ		지하철 → 지하철로
받침 O	+ 으로	젓가락 → 젓가락으로

e.g. 저는 학교에 버스로 가요.   김치를 젓가락으로 먹어요.

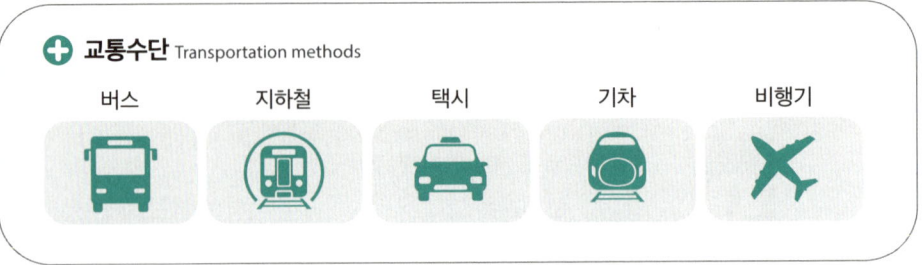

교통수단 Transportation methods

버스   지하철   택시   기차   비행기

어떻게 how   기차 train   지하철 subway   젓가락 chopsticks

A 회사에 어떻게 가요? How do you go to the office?
B 지하철로 가요 I go on the subway.

Culture

한국의 교통카드 Korea's transportation card

There are cards available in Korea for use on all major forms of public transportation. Perhaps the best-known of these public transportation cards is called the T-money card, which works both on the bus and the subway. Nowadays T-money is available not only in card format but also on mobile devices, bracelets, and keychains. You can even have a card custom-made with an image of your choice. A T-money card can be topped up at a convenience store, a card reload device at a subway station, or an ATM at a bank. In addition to covering public transit fares, T-money can also be spent like cash at supermarkets, bakeries, fast food restaurants, post offices, parking lots, and other locations.

QUIZ

1. Read the sentence and choose the correct form of the particle "(으)로."

1) 저는 컴퓨터(로 ☐ / 으로 ☐) 영화를 봐요.

2) 학교에 버스(로 ☐ / 으로 ☐) 가요.

3) 회사에서 한국말(로 ☐ / 으로 ☐) 말해요.

4) 저는 휴대전화(로 ☐ / 으로 ☐) 책을 읽어요.

5) 저는 젓가락(로 ☐ / 으로 ☐) 냉면을 먹어요.

A 기차표를 뭐로 샀어요? What did you buy your train ticket with?
   B 카드로 샀어요. I bought it with a credit card.

➕ **을/를 예매하다** To book

"예매하다" refers to making an advance purchase ("booking," in other words) of tickets or something similar.

e.g. 콘서트 표를 예매했어요.

➕ **을/를 예약하다** To make a reservation

"예약하다" refers to contacting an establishment such as a restaurant, doctor's office, or hairdresser's to make an appointment or reservation.

e.g. 식당을 예약했어요.

표 ticket   카드 (credit) card

A 비행기표를 어떻게 예매했어요? How did you book your plane ticket?
B 인터넷으로 예매했어요. I booked it on the Internet.

QUIZ

2. Look at the pictures and say what each of the following items are eaten with.

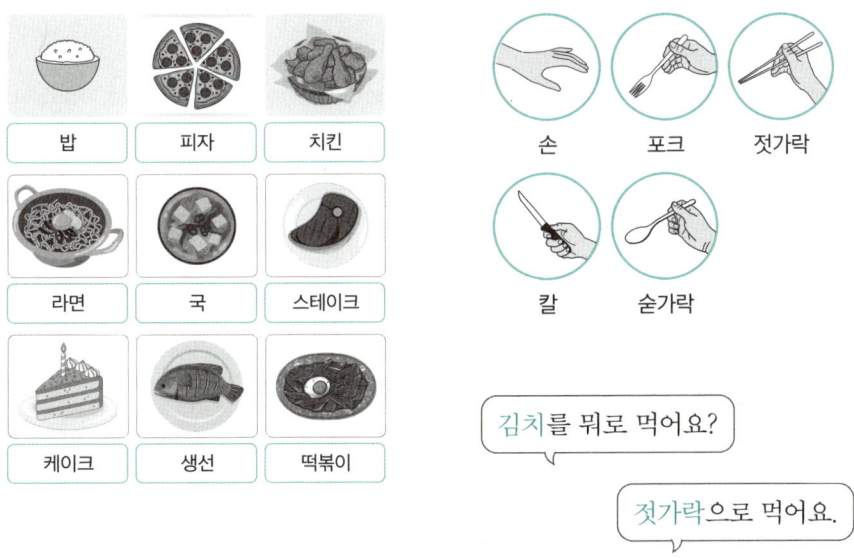

인터넷 internet   예매하다 to book   손 hand   포크 fork   칼 knife   숟가락 spoon
국 soup   스테이크 steak   케이크 cake

31 기차로 부산에 갈 거예요   137

32 부산까지 얼마나 걸려요?
How Long Does It Take to Get to Busan?

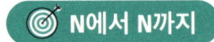

A 마리 씨는 어느 나라에서 왔어요? What country are you from, Marie?
B 저는 프랑스에서 왔어요. I'm from France.

마리 씨는 _____ _____ 왔어요? A
B 저는 _____ 왔어요.

N에서 N까지

These two particles are attached to nouns of location, with "에서" indicating the starting point and "까지" indicating the ending point. While they are generally used as a pair to express where movement begins and ends, they can also be used separately.

e.g. 저는 인도**에서** 왔어요.
　　 호텔**까지** 택시로 갈 거예요.

호텔 hotel

A 학교에서 집까지 어떻게 가요? How do you get home from school?
B 버스로 가요. I take the bus.

A 학교____ 집____ 어떻게 가요?
B 버스로 가요.

QUIZ

1. Look at the picture and complete the sentence with either "에서" and "까지" or both, as needed.

1)  안녕하세요? 저는 다니엘이에요. 독일____ 왔어요.

2)  이 기차는 서울역____ 가요.

3) 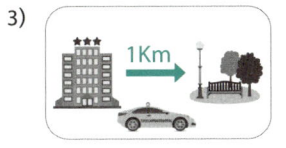 호텔____ 공원____ 택시로 가요.

4)  서울____ 부산____ 비행기로 갈 거예요.

A 학교에서 집까지 얼마나 걸려요? How long does it take to get home from school?
B 버스로 30분쯤 걸려요. It takes about 30 minutes on the bus.

_분/_시간(이) 걸리다

- The verb "걸리다" is used to indicate the time it takes to do something. When talking about time in this way, minutes (분) are counted with Sino-Korean numbers (일, 이, 삼, 사, etc.) and hours (시간) are counted with pure Korean numbers (한, 두, 세, 네, etc.).

    e.g. 집까지 **삼 분** 걸려요.   부산까지 **세 시간** 걸려요.

- "(으)로" can be used along with this grammar construction to express both the transportation method and the time spent in transit.

    e.g. **버스로** 10분쯤 걸려요

Culture

전주 한옥 마을 Jeonju Hanok Village

Located in Jeonju, North Jeolla Province, Jeonju Hanok Village is home to the largest collection of hanok (traditional Korean houses) in Korea, with over 700 hanok clustered together. Some of these houses date back to the Joseon Dynasty, while others are more modern. Visitors can fully enjoy the village's charm by strolling through its quiet alleys, especially on weekdays when it is less crowded. Staying overnight in a hanok offers a unique cultural experience, along with the chance to try Jeonju's famous bibimbap. For an even more immersive experience, visitors can rent a hanbok (traditional Korean attire) from nearby shops. A popular photo spot is Gyeonggijeon Shrine, where you can pose in front of its beautiful tiled roofs and walls. The shrine also houses a portrait of King Taejo, the founder of the Joseon Dynasty.

얼마나 how long

A 서울에서 부산까지 비행기로 얼마나 걸려요?
How long does it take to get from Seoul to Busan on a plane?

B 한 시간쯤 걸려요. It takes about one hour.

Listen to the recording and respond with your own information.

서울에서 고향까지 비행기로 얼마나 걸려요?

QUIZ

2. Look at the picture and complete the dialogue.

1) 회사 — 15분 — 집
A: _____ 얼마나 걸려요?
B: _____.

2) 호텔 — 40분 — 공항
A: _____ 얼마나 걸려요?
B: _____.

3) 서울 — 2시간 — 전주
A: _____ 얼마나 걸려요?
B: _____.

33 집에 걸어서 가요
I Go Home on Foot

A 학교에 어떻게 가요? How do you go to school?
B 걸어서 가요. I go on foot.

학교에 어떻게 _____? A
B _____ 가요.

Irregular "ㄷ"

When certain irregular "ㄷ" verbs such as "듣다" and "걷다" take a verb ending that begins with a vowel, the "ㄷ" changes to "ㄹ."

	-아요/어요	-(으)세요	-았어요/었어요	-고	-지만	-(으)ㄹ 거예요	-(으)려고 해요
듣다	들어요	들으세요	들었어요	듣고	듣지만	들을 거예요	들으려고 해요
걷다	걸어요	걸으세요	걸었어요	걷고	걷지만	걸을 거예요	걸으려고 해요

e.g. 저는 휴대폰으로 음악을 **들어요**.

> ➕ **교통수단 + 타요 / 타고 가요** Transportation methods + taking to go
>
> - Below are some of the ways to say which means of transportation you are taking to go somewhere.
>
>   e.g. A: 부산에 어떻게 가요?
>   B: ① 버스로 가요. (O)   ② 버스를 타요. (O)   ③ 버스를 타고 가요. (O)
>
> - When the location appears in the sentence, it should be followed by, "타고 가요."
>
>   e.g. 부산에 버스를 **타요**. (X) → 부산에 버스를 **타고 가요**. (O)

음악 music

A 학교까지 걸어서 얼마나 걸려요? How long does it take to get to school on foot?
B 15분쯤 걸려요. It takes about 15 minutes.

➕ **걸어서 가요** On foot

This expression is used to say that you get to a certain location by walking (that is, "on foot"). "걷다" and "-아서/어서" combine as "걸어서."

e.g. A: 시장에 어떻게 가요?
　　 B: 걸어서 가요.

UIZ

1. Look at the picture and complete the dialogue.

1)
A: 카페까지 어떻게 가요?
B: _____.
A: 얼마나 걸려요?
B: _____.

2)
A: 학교에서 병원까지 어떻게 갔어요?
B: _____.
A: 얼마나 걸렸어요?
B: _____.

쯤 about, approximately

33 집에 걸어서 가요

A 어제 무슨 운동을 했어요? What exercise did you do yesterday?
B 공원에서 한 시간쯤 걸었어요. I walked for about an hour in the park.

A: 어제 _____ 운동을 했어요?

B: 공원에서 _____.

QUIZ

2. Complete each dialogue by correctly conjugating the irregular "ㄷ" verb.

1) A: 지금 뭐 해요?
   B: 음악을 _____.
   (듣다 + -아요/어요)

2) A: 어제 뭐 했어요?
   B: 공원에서 _____ 커피를 마셨어요.
   (걷다 + -고)

3) A: 어제 뭐 했어요?
   B: 유튜브를 보고 한국 노래를 _____.
   (듣다 + -았어요/었어요)

4) A: 오후에 뭘 하려고 해요?
   B: 밥을 먹고 _____.
   (걷다 + -(으)려고 해요)

5) A: 저녁에 보통 뭐 해요?
   B: 뉴스를 _____ 책을 읽어요.
   (듣다 + -거나)

A 지하철에서 뭘 해요? What do you do in the subway?
B 유튜브를 보거나 음악을 들어요. I watch YouTube or listen to music.

A: _____ 뭘 해요?
B: 유튜브를 _____ 음악을 _____.

Culture

한국의 대중교통 Public transit in Korea

One aspect of Korean culture that is often a pleasant surprise for foreign visitors is public transit. Korean public transit is regarded as highly reliable and convenient: facilities are clean, service is quick, Wi-Fi is free, and traffic can be monitored in real time on your mobile device. There's also a transfer benefit program in place that enables passengers to move freely between subways and buses and get discounts on transfer fees, too. Transfer benefits are only available for 30 minutes after getting off the bus or train, and only when using a public transportation card. Since discounts are calculated by the card reader, don't forget to tap your card on the reader when you disembark.

34 KTX가 아주 빨라요
The KTX Is Very Fast

Irregular "르"

A 서울에서 부산까지 KTX로 얼마나 걸려요?
How long does it take to go from Seoul to Busan on the KTX?
B 두 시간 정도 걸려요. It takes about two hours.
A 와! 아주 빨라요. Wow! That's really fast.

Irregular "르"

When a verb or adjective ending in "르" takes a verb ending that starts with "-아/어," the "ㅡ" is dropped and a "ㄹ" is added, turning the verb ending's first styllable into "-라/-러."

	-아요/어요	-았어요/었어요	-고	-지만	-(으)ㄹ 거예요
빠르다	빨라요	빨랐어요	빠르고	빠르지만	빠를 거예요
다르다	달라요	달랐어요	다르고	다르지만	다를 거예요
모르다	몰라요	몰랐어요	모르고	모르지만	모를 거예요
부르다	불러요	불렀어요	부르고	부르지만	부를 거예요
자르다	잘라요	잘랐어요	자르고	자르지만	자를 거예요

KTX(케이티엑스) Korea Train Express (high speed rail system)   **빠르다** to be fast
다르다 to be different   **모르다** to not know   **(노래를) 부르다** to sing   **자르다** to cut

A 저는 전에 부산에서 살았어요. I used to live in Busan.
B 오, 그래요? 몰랐어요. Oh, is that so? I didn't know that.

➕ **오, 그래요?** Oh, is that so?

Some expressions that are used to react to new information that comes up in conversation are: "오, 그래요?" (Oh, is that so?) "정말요?" (Really?) and "오, 몰랐어요" (Oh, I didn't know that).

UIZ

1. Complete the sentence by conjugating the given word.

1) KTX가 아주 _____. (빠르다)

2) 저는 중국어를 _____. (모르다)

3) 보통 미용실에서 머리를 _____. (자르다)

4) 다니엘 씨는 한국 노래를 잘 _____. (부르다)

그래요? Is that so?   머리 hair   잘 well

A 다니엘 씨는 한국 노래를 아주 잘 불러요. Daniel sings Korean songs very well.
B 그래요? 몰랐어요. Really? I didn't know that.

Culture

한국의 노래방 문화 Korea's karaoke culture

Koreans tend to be big fans of singing, which they regard, along with dancing, as a good way to unwind for people of all ages. For that reason, 노래방 (karaoke rooms) are a frequent sight in Korea. They're especially common near the restaurants and bars that cluster around university campuses and commercial districts. Office workers sometimes follow up a company dinner with a round of karaoke to promote good feelings with their colleagues. And students are known to drop by a 노래방 with friends to take a break from the daily grind or to share their feelings with a crush. Families often go on outings to a 노래방, and there are even single-occupancy 코인노래방 (coin-operated karaoke rooms) where people can go for some solitary singing practice.

A 다니엘 씨, 오늘 헤어스타일이 좀 달라요.
Daniel, your hairstyle looks a little different today.
B 어제 머리를 잘랐어요. I got a haircut yesterday.

QUIZ

2. Look at the picture and complete the dialogue.

1)

A: 어제 뭐 했어요?
B: 쇼핑하고 머리를 _____.

2)

A: 어제 뭐 했어요?
B: 밥을 먹고 노래방에서 노래를 _____.

3)

A: 노래방에서 무슨 노래를 부를 거예요?
B: 한국 노래를 _____.

4)

A: 주말에 뭐 하려고 해요?
B: 미용실에서 머리를 _____.

헤어스타일 hairstyle

35 머리가 아파요
My Head Hurts

 Dropping "ㅡ"

A 어디가 아파요? Where does it hurt?
B 머리가 아파요. My head hurts.

Dropping "ㅡ"

When adjectives or verbs with the final vowel "ㅡ" take an ending that starts with "-아/어," the "ㅡ" is dropped.

	-아요/어요	-(으)세요	-았어요/었어요	-고	-지만
아프다	아파요		아팠어요	아프고	아프지만
바쁘다	바빠요		바빴어요	바쁘고	바쁘지만
나쁘다	나빠요		나빴어요	나쁘고	나쁘지만
예쁘다	예뻐요		예뻤어요	예쁘고	예쁘지만
쓰다	써요	쓰세요	썼어요	쓰고	쓰지만

몸 (신체) The human body

아프다 to hurt, to be sick   바쁘다 to be busy   나쁘다 to be bad   예쁘다 to be pretty   쓰다 write
머리 head   눈 eye   코 nose   입 mouth   귀 ear   목 neck   가슴 chest   어깨 shoulder
팔 arm   손 hand   배 stomach   허리 back   다리 leg   무릎 knee   발 foot

A 어디가 아파요? Where does it hurt?
　　B 눈이 아파요. My eye hurts.

N이/가 아프다

- "이/가 아프다" is placed after a body part noun to express bodily pain.

| 받침 ✗ + 가 | 머리 → 머리가 | 받침 ○ + 이 | 눈 → 눈이 |

- The expression "어디가 아파요?" is used to ask which part of the body is in pain.
  - e.g. A: 어디가 아파요?   B: 목이 아파요.

QUIZ

1. Match each word to the appropriate body part.

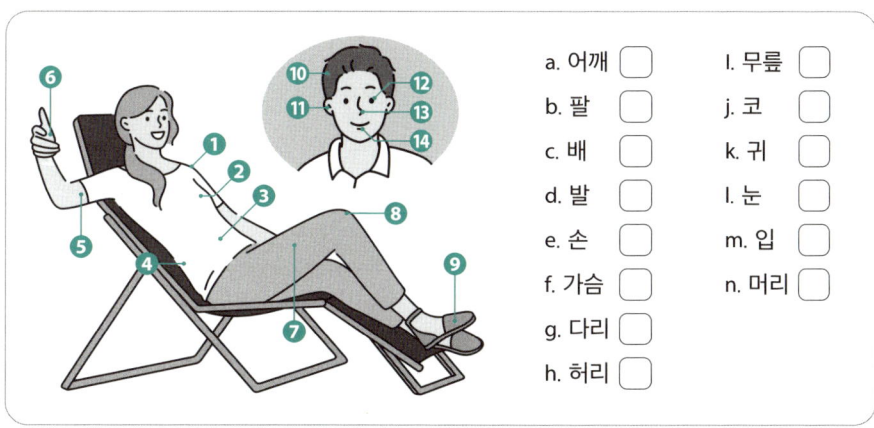

a. 어깨　　i. 무릎
b. 팔　　　j. 코
c. 배　　　k. 귀
d. 발　　　l. 눈
e. 손　　　m. 입
f. 가슴　　n. 머리
g. 다리
h. 허리

A 왜 그래요? What's the matter?
B 배가 너무 아파요. My stomach hurts so badly.

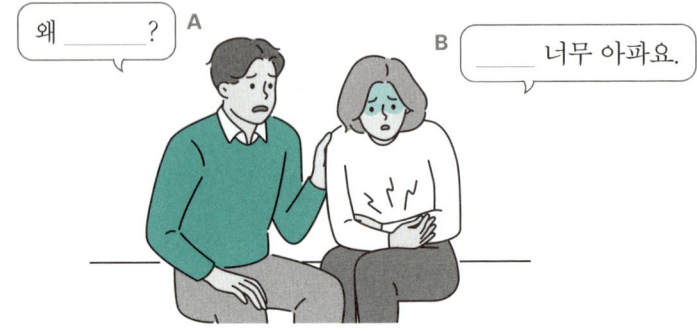

왜 _____ ? A
B _____ 너무 아파요.

➕ **왜 그래요?** What's wrong?

This expression is used to ask what's wrong with somebody.

 A: 왜 그래요?   B: 머리가 좀 아파요.

QUIZ

2. Look at the picture and answer which body part is hurting.

1)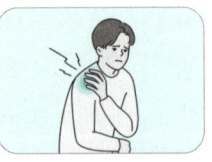

A: 어디가 아파요?
B: _____.

2)

A: 어디가 아파요?
B: _____.

3)

A: 어디가 아파요?
B: _____.

왜 why   너무 too (much)

A 토요일에 시간이 있어요? Are you free on Saturday?
B 아니요, 토요일에 바빠요. No, I'm busy on Saturday.

QUIZ

3. Read the dialogue and conjugate the verb correctly.

1) A: 내일 시간이 있어요?

   B: 아니요. 내일은 _____.(바쁘다 + -아요/어요)

2) A: 꽃이 어때요?

   B: 정말 _____.(예쁘다 + -아요/어요)

3) A: 지금 뭐 해요?

   B: 전화번호를 _____.(쓰다 + -아요/어요)

4) A: 어제 회사에 안 갔어요?

   B: 네. 머리가 _____.(아프다 + -았/었어요)

Culture

엄마 손이 약손 Mommy's healing hands

According to an old Korean proverb, a mother's hands are healing hands. Most Koreans have a childhood memory of their mother massaging their stomach during a tummy ache and singing the proverb "엄마 손이 약손." Remarkably enough, many children found that the massage brought relief from their stomachache. In fact, a stomach massage is said to have a real medicinal effect, easing pain by restarting digestive function and easing tension in the bowels. So the next time you have a stomachache, try massaging your stomach while singing those timeless words, "엄마 손이 약손."

시간 time, hour   꽃 flower

36 오늘 날씨가 추워요
The Weather Is Cold Today

 Irregular "ㅂ"

A 오늘 날씨가 어때요? How is the weather today?
B 따뜻하고 맑아요. It's warm and clear.

Irregular "ㅂ"

- When verbs and adjectives with final consonant "ㅂ" take an ending that starts with a vowel, the "ㅂ" turns into a "우."

	-아요/어요	-았어요/었어요	-고	-지만
춥다	추워요	추웠어요	춥고	춥지만
덥다	더워요	더웠어요	덥고	덥지만
맵다	매워요	매웠어요	맵고	맵지만
쉽다	쉬워요	쉬웠어요	쉽고	쉽지만
어렵다	어려워요	어려웠어요	어렵고	어렵지만

- "돕다" is an exception. If it takes an ending that starts with "-아/어," the "ㅂ" turns into an "오."

  e.g. 저는 친구를 **도와요**.

- A few verbs and adjectives including "입다" (to wear) and "좁다" (to be narrow) are conjugated regularly without exhibiting the changes explained above.

  e.g. 저는 치마를 자주 **입어요**.   길이 **좁아요**.

따뜻하다 to be warm   맑다 to be clear   춥다 to be cold   덥다 to be hot   맵다 to be spicy
쉽다 to be easy   어렵다 to be difficult   돕다 to help   좁다 to be narrow

A 오늘 날씨가 어때요? How is the weather today?
B 아주 추워요. It's very cold.

 Listen to the recording and respond with your own information.

날씨 Weather

| 맑다 | 흐리다 | 따뜻하다 | 시원하다 | 춥다 | 덥다 |

##

1. Complete the sentence by conjugating the provided word.

1) A: 이 김치가 어때요?
   B: 아주 _____.(맵다)

2) A: 오늘 날씨가 어때요?
   B: 아주 _____.(덥다)

3) A: 이 책이 쉬워요?
   B: 아니요, 좀 _____.(어렵다)

4) A: 오늘 날씨가 따뜻해요?
   B: 아니요, 좀 _____.(춥다)

시원하다 to be cool, refreshing   흐리다 to be cloudy

A 지금 일본은 날씨가 어때요? How is the weather in Japan right now?
B 춥고 흐려요. It's cold and cloudy.

A 지금 _____ 날씨가 어때요?
B _____ 흐려요.

➕ __은/는 날씨가 어때요? How is the weather in __?

This is used when talking about the weather in a specific city or country. The name of the city or country goes before "은/는."

e.g. 한국은 오늘 날씨가 추워요.
어제 제주도는 날씨가 따뜻했어요.

Culture

대구의 날씨 Daegu weather

The city of Daegu is widely known for having some of the hottest summer weather in Korea. Daegu's hot summers are largely due to its geography. The city is surrounded on all sides by mountains, which help retain heat within the city and prevent air circulation to other regions. Another reason for the heat buildup is that Daegu is a highly urbanized and densely populated metropolis. It is also located in a sunny part of the country that is famous for its delicious apples. In short, Daegu has both natural and urban factors that contribute to its high average temperatures. Because of these weather conditions, Daegu has earned the nickname "대프리카," a portmanteau of "대구" (Daegu) and "아프리카" (Africa). This humorous term is used to emphasize how hot the city can get in the summer. Koreans often associate Africa with hot weather, which is why the name was created. However, it is important to note that the nickname is simply a way to describe Daegu's climate and is not meant to refer to the actual climate of the African continent.

A 어제 대구는 날씨가 어땠어요? How was the weather in Daegu yesterday?
B 아주 더웠어요. It was very hot.

A: 어제 대구는 날씨가 _____?
B: 아주 _____.

QUIZ

2. Look at the picture and complete the dialogue.

1) A: 오늘 서울은 날씨가 어때요?
   B: 아주 더워요.

2) A: 오늘 전주____ 날씨가 어때요?
   B: _____.

3) A: 오늘 제주도____ 날씨가 어때요?
   B: _____.

37 어느 계절을 좋아해요?
Which Season Do You Like?

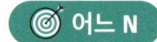 어느 N

A 어느 계절을 좋아해요? Which season do you like?
B 저는 봄을 좋아해요. I like spring.

_____ 좋아해요? A
B 저는 _____ 좋아해요.

어느 + N

This is used to ask "which" something is, while having a distinct group of two or more things in mind.

발음 Pronunciation

"계절" can be pronounced [계절] or [게절].

e.g. 계절 [계절 / 게절]

계절 Season

봄   여름   가을   겨울

e.g. 한국에는 **사계절**이 있어요.   저는 **여름**에 여행을 가요.

계절 season   봄 spring   여름 summer   가을 fall   겨울 winter

50일 완성 한국어 1

A 어느 식당에서 밥을 먹어요? Which restaurant are you eating at?
B 중국 식당에서 먹어요. I'm eating at the Chinese restaurant.

_____ 밥을 먹어요? A   B _____ 먹어요.

QUIZ

1. Match the Korean and English words for the seasons.

1) 봄 • • winter
2) 여름 • • fall
3) 가을 • • spring
4) 겨울 • • summer

2. Provide appropriate answers for the following questions.

1) A: 어느 계절을 좋아해요?
   B: _____.

2) A: 어느 나라 사람이에요?
   B: _____.

3) A: 어느 식당에서 밥을 자주 먹어요?
   B: _____.

자주 often

A 어느 나라 사람이에요? What is your nationality?
B 저는 독일 사람이에요. I'm German.

A: _____ _____ 사람이에요?
B: _____ 사람이에요.

➕ 무슨 vs. 어느 What (kind of) vs. Which

- "무슨" is used in the sense of "what kind of" when asking about something you don't know about.

    e.g. A: **무슨** 과일을 사요?   B: 사과를 사요.

- "어느" is used to ask "which" something is, while having a distinct group of two or more things in mind.

    e.g. A: **어느** 과일을 사요?   B: 사과를 사요.

✅ QUIZ

3. Complete each sentence with either "무슨" or "어느."

> 무슨 / 어느

1) A: 오늘이 (   ) 요일이에요?
   B: 금요일이에요.

2) A: (   ) 선생님이 한국어를 가르쳐요?
   B: 김 선생님이 가르쳐요.

3) A: 냉장고에 사과 주스하고 포도 주스가 있어요.
   B: (   ) 주스가 맛있어요?

4) A: (   ) 아르바이트를 해요?
   B: 저는 식당에서 일해요.

5) A: (   ) 운동을 해요?
   B: 축구를 해요.

6) A: (   ) 나라 사람이에요?
   B: 독일 사람이에요.

A 어느 회사에 다녀요? Which company do you work for?
B 한국컴퓨터에 다녀요. I work for Korea Computers.

➕ -에 다니다 To attend (school) / To work at (a company)

The expression "-에 다니다," which literally means "going somewhere frequently," is often used to mean "attending" a school or "working at" a company.

e.g. 저는 회사에 다녀요.
저는 하나대학교에 다녀요.

Culture

한국의 계절 음식 Seasonal foods of Korea

Korea has seasonal foods that are typically enjoyed in certain types of weather. 냉면 (cold noodles), a North Korean specialty, used to be eaten frequently in the winter to keep cool on the toasty 온돌 (heated) floor. But since ice is widely available now, refreshing 물냉면 is nowadays often eaten in the hot summer months. Another summer specialty is 빙수, or shaved ice. 빙수 has traditionally been eaten with 인절미 or other kinds of rice cake, but these days strawberries, melons, mangos, and green teas are all popular 빙수 toppings. Despite 삼계탕 (chicken soup with ginseng) being a hot dish, it's frequently eaten in the sweltering summer months because it's considered a tonic that can keep you healthy in the heat. In the cold winter months, Koreans often snack on street foods like fish cake, roasted sweet potatoes, roasted chestnuts, 호빵, 호떡, and 붕어빵. "붕어빵" literally means "carp bread," though it contains no fish. Rather, it's a fish-shaped pastry that's stuffed with treats such as red beans, custard cream, and seeds. What kinds of seasonal foods do you have in your home country?

38 추워서 겨울을 안 좋아해요

A/V-아서/어서

I Don't Like Winter Because It's Cold

A 왜 봄을 좋아해요? Why do you like the spring?
B 날씨가 따뜻해서 봄을 좋아해요. I like the spring because the weather is warm.

A ___ 봄을 좋아해요?
B _____ 봄을 좋아해요.

A/V-아서/어서 1

This combines with a verb or adjective to express the reason or grounds for something. When the verb or adjective's final vowel is "ㅏ, ㅗ," "아서" is placed at the end. When the verb or adjective ends in "하다," "-해서" is placed at the end. And when the verb or adjective does not have a final vowel of "ㅏ, ㅗ" and does not end in "-하다," "어서" is placed at the end.

ㅏ, ㅗ + -아서			-하다 → -해서		in all other cases + -어서		
비싸다	+-아서	→ 비싸서	따뜻하다	→ 따뜻해서	멀다	+-어서	→ 멀어서
많다		→ 많아서	피곤하다	→ 피곤해서	재미있다		→ 재미있어서
좋다		→ 좋아서	일하다	→ 일해서	크다		→ 커서
바쁘다		→ 바빠서	청소하다	→ 청소해서	춥다		→ 추워서

많다 to be a lot

A 겨울을 좋아해요? Do you like the winter?
B 아니요, 너무 추워서 겨울을 안 좋아해요.
No, I don't like the winter because it's cold.

A/V-아서/어서 2

This grammar construction cannot be followed by verbs that are propositive (making a suggestion) or imperative (giving a command). The grammar construction that comes before those verbs is "-(으)니까."

e.g. 이 책이 재미있어서 이 책을 읽으세요. (✕)
　　　이 책이 **재미있으니까** 이 책을 읽으세요. (○)

QUIZ

1. Complete the dialogue using the provided word.

1) A: 왜 가방을 안 사요?
　　B: _____. (비싸다)

2) A: 오늘 왜 일찍 집에 가요?
　　B: _____. (피곤하다)

3) A: 요즘 왜 친구를 안 만나요?
　　B: _____. (바쁘다)

일찍 early

A 토요일에 산에 갔어요? Did you go to the mountain on Saturday?
B 아니요, 비가 많이 와서 안 갔어요. No, there was a lot of rain so I didn't go.

A/V-아서/어서 3

The past tense marker "-았/었" is not used before "-아서/어서."

e.g. 어제 비가 많이 왔어요. + 산에 안 갔어요.
→ 어제 비가 많이 **와서** 산에 안 갔어요.

Culture

봄바람 A spring breeze

"봄바람" literally means the wind that blows in the spring, but the word has another meaning. As the weather grows warm in the spring and activities move outdoors, people often get excited about the prospect of meeting someone new. So "봄바람" is also used metaphorically to refer to the thrill of romance in the springtime. When you're listening to Korean popular songs, you may sometimes encounter lyrics that compare the passion of love to the spring breeze.

A 어제 뭐 했어요? What did you do yesterday?
B 너무 더워서 하루 종일 집에 있었어요.
It was so hot that I stayed at home all day long.

QUIZ

2. Look at the picture and complete the dialogue.

1)

A: 왜 여행을 안 갔어요?
B: _____ 안 갔어요.

2)

A: 어제 왜 학교에 안 갔어요?
B: _____ 안 갔어요.

3)

A: 배불러요?
B: 네, _____ 배불러요.

4)

A: 피곤해요?
B: 아니요, _____ 안 피곤해요.

하루 종일 all day long

39 눈이 많이 와서 산에 못 갔어요
It Snowed a Lot, So I Couldn't Go to the Mountain

A 어제 산에 갔어요? Did you go to the mountain yesterday?
B 아니요, 못 갔어요. No, I couldn't go.

 못 V

"못" is used to indicate that the subject isn't able to perform the action of the verb.

e.g.
A: 점심 먹었어요?
B: 아니요, 바빠서 못 먹었어요.

A: 운동했어요?
B: 아니요, 다리가 아파서 못 했어요.

QUIZ

1. Complete the answers using the word "못."

1) A: 주말에 친구를 만났어요?
   B: 아니요, 바빠서 _____.

2) A: 한국에서 운전해요?
   B: 아니요, 차가 없어서 _____.

3) A: 가방을 샀어요?
   B: 아니요, 너무 비싸서 _____.

4) A: 어제 운동했어요?
   B: 아니요, 날씨가 추워서 _____.

A 왜 산에 못 갔어요? Why couldn't you go to the mountain?
B 눈이 와서 못 갔어요. I couldn't go because it snowed.

A: ___ 산에 ___?
B: ___ 와서 ___ 갔어요.

➕ 눈이 오다 / 비가 오다 It snows / it rains

- Koreans say "눈이 오다" to mean "it snows" and "비가 오다" to mean "it rains."
  - e.g. 지금 눈이 와요.   어제 비가 왔어요.

- The word "날씨가" is not used before "눈이 오다" or "비가 오다."
  - e.g. A: 날씨가 어때요?
    B: 날씨가 추워요. (O) = 추워요. (O)
    날씨가 더워요. (O) = 더워요. (O)
  - e.g. A: 날씨가 어때요?
    B: 날씨가 비가 와요. (X) / 비가 와요. (O)
    날씨가 눈이 와요. (X) / 눈이 와요. (O)

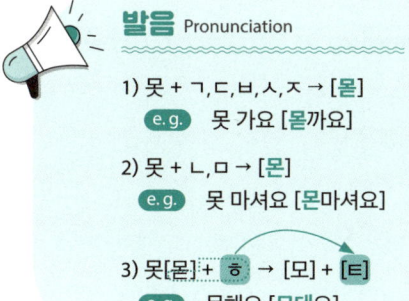

발음 Pronunciation

1) 못 + ㄱ,ㄷ,ㅂ,ㅅ,ㅈ → [몯]
   e.g. 못 가요 [몯까요]

2) 못 + ㄴ,ㅁ → [몬]
   e.g. 못 마셔요 [몬마셔요]

3) 못[몯] + ㅎ → [모] + [ㅌ]
   e.g. 못해요 [모태요]

✏ QUIZ

2. Look at the picture and answer the question about the weather.

1) A: 오늘 날씨가 어때요?
   B: _____.

2) A: 오늘 날씨가 어때요?
   B: _____.

눈 snow   눈이 오다 it snows   비 rain   비가 오다 it rains

A 오늘 친구를 만나요? Are you meeting your friend today?
B 아니요, 바빠서 못 만나요. No, I can't meet them because I'm busy.

➕ 못 V vs. 안 A/V

- "못" is placed in front of a verb to indicate that the subject isn't able to perform the action of the verb.
- "안" is placed in front of an adjective or verb to make the sentence negative.
  - e.g. 돈이 없어서 옷을 **못 사요**.   날씨가 **안 추워요**.   내일 학교에 **안 가요**.

✓UIZ

2. Choose the correct word to complete the sentence.

1) 오늘은 (못 ☐ / 안 ☐) 바빠요.
2) 태권도를 안 배워서 태권도를 (안 ☐ / 못 ☐)해요.
3) 주말에 수업이 없어서 학교에 (안 ☐ / 못 ☐) 가요.
4) 약을 먹어서 머리가 (안 ☐ / 못 ☐) 아파요.
5) 지금 비가 (못 ☐ / 안 ☐) 와요.
6) 친구 집에 갔지만 친구가 없어서 (안 ☐ / 못 ☐) 만났어요.

약 medicine   태권도 taekwondo

A 태권도를 했어요? Did you do taekwondo?
B 아니요, 다리가 아파서 못 했어요. No, I couldn't because my leg was hurting.

A _____ 했어요?
B 아니요, _____ 아파서 __ 했어요.

Culture

태권도 Taekwondo

Taekwondo, Korea's national sport, is a martial art that largely relies on kicking techniques and can be used to effectively overpower an adversary with the hands, feet, and other body parts. This martial art became an official Olympic sport in the 2000 Sydney Olympics. Korean students often study taekwondo at private academies given its focus on teaching good manners and good character. As taekwondo practitioners advance in rank, their belt color changes through five stages: white, yellow, blue, red, and black. Belt  promotion tests are administered by a state-run organization called Kukkiwon, also known as the World Taekwondo Headquarters. Many Korean men end up learning taekwondo during their mandatory military service if they haven't already learned it before. Soldiers who do particularly well in their taekwondo training can sometimes receive extra leave. It's worth trying out taekwondo, which can impart both physical and mental strength.

40 누구의 가방이에요?
Whose Bag Is It?

 A 이거는 누구의 모자예요? Whose cap is this?
B 다니엘 씨의 모자예요. It's Daniel's cap.

 N의 1

This is placed between two nouns to show that the preceding noun has possession over the following noun.

받침 X	+ 의	친구의 가방
받침 O		선생님의 가방

 **발음** 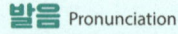 Pronunciation

"의" must be pronounced as [의] when it appears in the first syllable of a word. But it can also be pronounced as [ㅣ] when it appears in other syllables and as [ㅔ] when it is used as a particle.

 의사 [의사]   의자 [의자]
회의 [회의/회이]   강의실 [강의실/강이실]
수진 씨의 가방 [수진 씨의 가방/수진 씨에 가방]

A 이거는 누구의 가방이에요? Whose bag is this?
B 선생님의 가방이에요. It's the teacher's bag.

QUIZ

1. Look at the picture and complete the dialogue.

1)

A: 이거는 누구의 가방이에요?
B: 다니엘의 가방이에요   .

2)

A: 이거는 누구의 자전거예요?
B: _____.

3)

A: 이거는 누구의 볼펜이에요?
B: _____.

4)

A: 이거는 누구의 구두예요?
B: _____.

구두 dress shoes

A 다니엘 씨, 이거는 누구의 가방이에요? Daniel, whose bag is this?
B 선생님, 이거는 제 가방이에요. It's my (humble form) bag.

다니엘 씨, 이거는 _____ _____ 이에요? A

B 선생님, 이거는 ____ ____이에요.

N의 2

- The particle "의" can be dropped.

  e.g. 누구의 가방이에요? = 누구 가방이에요?
  다니엘 씨의 가방이에요. = 다니엘 씨 가방이에요.

- "저의" (the humble form of "my") can be contracted to "제," and "나의" (the plain form of "my") can be contracted to "내."

  e.g. 저의 가방 = 제 가방
  나의 가방 = 내 가방

Culture

저 vs. 나 Korean forms of "I/me"

Korean has two forms of the first person pronoun ("I/me"), with their usage depending on the person being spoken to. When the other person is older or of higher status than the speaker, the humble form "저" is used. But when the other person is of equal or lower status to the speaker, the plain form "나" is used.

A 다니엘 씨, 이거는 누구 가방이에요? Daniel, whose bag is this?
B 미나 씨, 이거는 내 가방이에요. It's my (plain form) bag

다니엘 씨, 이거는 _____ ____이에요? A

B 미나 씨, 이거는 __ ____이에요.

QUIZ

2. Look at the picture and complete the dialogue.

1)

A: 수진 씨, 이거 수진 씨의 공책이에요?
B: 네, _____.

2)

A: 수진 씨, 이거 수진 씨의 우산이에요?
B: 아니요, 이거는 _____.

3)

A: 수진 씨, 이거 수진 씨의 시계예요?
B: 네, _____.

4)

A: 수진 씨, 이거 수진 씨의 휴대폰이에요?
B: 아니요, 이거는 _____.

공책 notebook

동생한테 선물을 보내려고 해요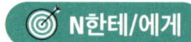
I'm Planning to Send a Present to My Younger Sibling

A 왜 우체국에 가요? Why are you going to the post office?
B 동생한테 선물을 보내려고 해요.
I'm planning to send a present to my younger sibling.

 **N한테**

"한테" is placed after an animate noun (a person or animal) to show that it's the beneficiary of the action of the sentence (also called the indirect object).

받침 X		친구**한테**
받침 O	+ 한테	동생**한테**

e.g. 저는 학생**한테** 태권도를 가르쳐요.
고양이**한테** 밥을 줬어요.

QUIZ

1. Fill in each blank with the correct particle below.

| 이/가 | 을/를 | 하고 | 에 | 에서 | 한테 |

1) 오늘 저녁(　　) 친구 결혼식에 가요.　2) 내일 약속(　　) 없어요.
3) 백화점 3층(　　) 구두가 있어요.　4) 밥을 집(　　) 먹어요.
5) 백화점에서 옷(　　) 샀어요.　6) 저는 동생(　　) 같이 운동했어요.
7) 아파서 병원(　　) 갔어요.　8) 내 생일에 친구가 나(　　) 선물을 줬어요.

우체국 post office   동생 younger sibling   선물 present, gift   고양이 cat   결혼식 wedding

A 누구한테 전화했어요? Who did you call?
B 선생님께 전화했어요. I called my teacher

_____ 전화했어요? A B _____ 전화했어요.

누구?

➕ 한테 < 께 Indicating the beneficiary

"께" is the honorific form of the particles "한테/에게." It's used when the beneficiary of the action (that is, the indirect object) is older or of higher status than the person doing the action.

e.g. 저는 선생님께 전화했어요.

Culture

한국의 결혼식 문화 Korean wedding culture

While Korean weddings are sometimes held at a church or hotel, the most common venue is a wedding hall, called a 예식장 in Korean. A ceremony at a wedding hall usually lasts for about an hour, with an emcee presiding and an officiant delivering a homily. The officiant is usually a respected figure chosen by the bride and groom. At Korean weddings, the mother of the bride wears pink hanbok (a traditional Korean outfit), while the mother of the groom wears blue hanbok. Wedding guests are expected to bring a monetary gift. The typical amount is 50,000 won, although a close friend may give 100,000 won or even more. Upon arriving at the venue, guests make their way to the bride or groom's reception desk, where they write their name on the register and deliver their monetary gift in exchange for a meal voucher. They then enter the chapel for the ceremony, which is followed by group photos on stage. Finally, they proceed to the prearranged restaurant to present their voucher and enjoy their meal. How different are Korean wedding customs from those of your country?

A 책을 누구에게 줬어요? Who did you give the book to?
B 친구에게 줬어요. I gave it to my friend.

"에게" means the same thing as "한테" but is a more literary expression. As such, it's mostly used in writing, and not very much in everyday conversation.

e.g. 저는 친구에게 책을 보내려고 해요.

A 어디에 전화했어요? Where did you call?
B 학교에 전화했어요. I called the school.

➕ N에게 vs. N에 To + (person or animal) vs. To + (place)

The particle "에" is used instead of "한테/에게/께" when the indirect object is a place, rather than a person or animal.

e.g. A: 이 소포를 어디에 보내려고 해요?
B: 미국에 보내려고 해요.

✅UIZ

2. Fill in each blank with the correct particle below.

> 한테   께   에

1) 저는 동생(   ) 편지를 썼어요.
2) 미나 씨는 아버지(   ) 선물을 보냈어요.
3) 나는 개(   ) 물을 줬어요.
4) 동생은 선생님(   ) 인사했어요.
5) 린데만 씨는 독일(   ) 전화했어요.

소포 package   인사하다 to greet

42 친구한테서 꽃을 받았어요
I Got Flowers from a Friend

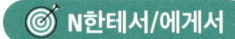 N한테서/에게서

A 와! 꽃이 예뻐요. 누구한테서 받았어요?
Wow, those flowers are pretty. Who did you get them from?

B 친구한테서 받았어요. I got them from a friend.

N한테서/에게서 1

- The particle "한테서" is placed after an animate noun (a person or animal) to indicate that the speaker has received something from them. It's mainly used with such verbs as "받다" (to receive), "배우다" (to learn), "듣다" (to listen), and "빌리다" (to borrow).

  e.g. 한국 친구한테서 그 이야기를 들었어요.
  다니엘 씨한테서 책을 빌리려고 해요.

- The particle "한테서" can be replaced with "에게서," which is generally used in the spoken language.

  e.g. 친구한테서 선물을 받았어요. = 친구에게서 선물을 받았어요.

- "한테서/에게서" cannot be used when the speaker has received something from a place or organization, rather than a person or animal. The particle "에서" is used in those cases.

  e.g. 병원에서 전화를 받았어요.
  도서관에서 책을 빌릴 거예요.

꽃 flower   받다 to receive, get   빌리다 to borrow

A 누구한테서 책을 빌렸어요? Who did you borrow the book from?
B 다니엘 씨한테서 빌렸어요. I borrowed it from Daniel.

✅QUIZ

1. Look at the picture and complete the sentence.

1)  _____ 꽃을 받았어요.

2) 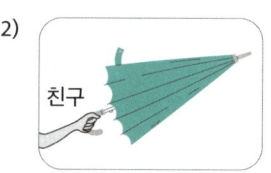 _____ 우산을 빌렸어요.

3)  _____ 이야기를 들었어요.

고향 hometown

A 생일에 친구들한테 선물을 많이 받았어요?
Did you get a lot of presents from your friends on your birthday?

B 네, 많이 받았어요. Yes, I got a lot of presents.

A: 생일에 _____ 선물을 많이 받았어요?

B: 네, _____ 받았어요.

💡 N한테서/에게서 2

The "서" in the particles "한테서/에게서" is sometimes omitted in colloquial language. But even without "서," the meaning is easy to figure out from the verbs in context.

A: 유나 씨는 누구한테 꽃을 줬어요?
B: 친구한테 꽃을 줬어요.

A: 유나 씨는 누구한테(서) 꽃을 받았어요?
B: 친구한테(서) 꽃을 받았어요.

Culture

연인들의 기념일 Romantic Celebrations for Couples

The most significant romantic day for Korean couples is Valentine's Day on February 14. In North America and Europe, it is customary for romantic partners to exchange flowers and gifts on this day. However, in Korea and Japan, Valentine's Day is when women give chocolates and express their feelings, following the widely accepted idea that it is a day for women to make the first move. Another important romantic day for Korean couples is White Day, celebrated on March 14. On this day, men express their love by giving candy, flowers, or other gifts in return. Do you have any special romantic days in your country?

A 한국어를 누구한테 처음 배웠어요? Who did you learn Korean from at first?
B 한국 친구한테 처음 배웠어요. I learned it from a Korean friend at first.

A 한국어를 _____ 처음 배웠어요?
B 한국 친구한테 처음 배웠어요.
한국 친구

 Listen to the recording and respond with your own information.

한국어를 누구한테 처음 배웠어요?

QUIZ

2. Complete each sentence with one of the particles below. Each particle will only be used once.

> 에   에서   에게   에게서

1) 내일 저는 친구 집(   ) 갈 거예요..
2) 저는 내일 의사(   ) 전화를 하려고 해요.
3) 한국 친구(   ) 한국어 책을 빌리려고 해요.
4) 어제 오후에 병원(   ) 전화를 받았어요.

42 친구한테서 꽃을 받았어요   **181**

43 옷을 사러 백화점에 갈 거예요
I'm Going to Go to the Department Store to Buy Clothes

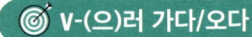

A 내일 뭐 할 거예요? What are you going to do tomorrow?

B 옷을 사러 백화점에 갈 거예요.
I'm going to go to the department store to buy clothes.

내일 ___ 할 거예요?   A

B   옷을 ___ 백화점에 ___ ___.

V-(으)러 가다/오다

- This expression is used to express the reason for going somewhere.
- "V-(으)러" is followed by a verb of movement (가다, 오다, 다니다, etc.).

받침 X	+ 러	사다 → 사러
받침 ㄹ		만들다 → 만들러
받침 O	+ 으러	먹다 → 먹으러

A 어디에 가요? Where are you going?
B 식당에 밥 먹으러 가요. I'm going to a restaurant to eat a meal.

QUIZ

1. Provide appropriate answers for the following questions.

1)

A: 어디에 가요?

B: _____(으)러 도서관에 가요.

2)

A: 어디에 가요?

B: _____(으)러 영화관에 가요.

3)

A: 왜 카페에 갔어요?

B: _____(으)러 갔어요.

4)

A: 왜 시장에 갔어요?

B: _____(으)러 갔어요.

A 요즘 운동해요? Are you exercising these days?
B 네, 스포츠센터에 운동하러 다녀요. Yes, I go to the fitness center to exercise.

A 요즘 _____?
B 네, 스포츠센터에 _____ _____.

QUIZ

2. Choose the correct expression for each sentence.

1) 옷을 (사서☐ / 사러☐) 백화점에 가요.

2) 비행기를 (타서☐ / 타러☐) 공항에 가요.

3) 비가 (와서☐ / 오러☐) 우산을 샀어요.

4) 꽃을 (사서☐ / 사러☐) 꽃집에 갔어요.

5) 많이 (걸어서☐ / 걸으러☐) 다리가 아파요.

6) 친구 집에 (놀아서☐ / 놀러☐) 가요.

스포츠센터 fitness center   공항 airport   놀다 to hang out

A 어제 뭐 했어요? What did you do yesterday?
B 친구가 우리 집에 놀러 왔어요. A friend came by my house to hang out.

Culture

우리 N Mine and Ours

In Korea, the word "우리" (our) is often used where one might expect to hear "나의" (my). "우리" is used to communicate a close relationship with someone or something when the listener is not of higher status. A Korean living on their own is still apt to say, "여기가 우리 집이에요" (this is "our" house) rather than "여기가 내 집이에요" (this is "my" house). An only child will refer to their mother as "우리 엄마," not "내 엄마," and a wife will even speak of her husband not as "남편" or "내 남편" but as "우리 남편." When talking about one's wife in Korean, it's typical to say "우리 아내" or "우리 와이프," borrowing the word from English. That should spare you the shock of hearing a Korean talking about "우리 남편"!

44 같이 저녁을 먹을래요?
Would You Like to Have Dinner with Me?

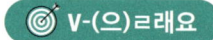 V-(으)ㄹ래요

 A 커피 마실래요? Would you like to drink some coffee?
B 네, 마실래요. Yes, I would.

V-(으)ㄹ래요 1

- This grammar construction is used to express the speaker's intentions or to ask about the listener's intentions.

받침 X	+ ㄹ래요	갈래요
받침 ㄹ		만들래요
받침 O	+ 을래요	읽을래요

- This is generally used in informal speech.
  - e.g. A: 커피 마실래요?
    B: 아니요, 안 마실래요.

- Since this must be used to either express the speaker's intentions (first person) or ask about the listener's intentions (second person), it can't be used with a third person subject.

A 뭐 먹을래요? What would you like to eat?
B 저는 냉면을 먹을래요. I would like to eat some naengmyeon.

A 뭐 _____?

B 저는 냉면을 _____.

QUIZ

1. Look at the picture and use "-(으)ㄹ래요" to complete the sentence.

1)  피곤해서 내일 저는 집에서 _____.

2)  토요일에 집에서 책을 _____.

3)  오늘 저는 집에 일찍 _____.

A 토요일에 같이 저녁을 먹을래요?
Would you like to have dinner with me on Saturday?

B 네, 좋아요. Yes, I would.

A 토요일에 _____ _____ ?
B 네, _____.

V-(으)ㄹ래요 2

This grammar construction can also be used to ask the listener whether they would like to do something together with the speaker. In this sense of making a suggestion, the grammar construction is sometimes accompanied by expressions such as "우리" and "같이."

Culture

한국인의 커피 사랑 Koreans' love of coffee

Koreans are unusually fond of coffee. It's very common to grab some coffee after lunch, and office workers in business districts can often be seen doing that around their office after lunch. One market research company found that Korea had the third-most coffee shops in the world in 2019, after the United States and China. Korea also ranked third in the yearly average of café spending per capita (104,000 won). Until foreign café franchises reached the country in 1999, Koreans generally drank instant coffee mixes. Since then, franchises have proliferated, and many people have purchased coffee machines for home use. Today, Koreans drink various kinds of coffee, and not just instant coffee mixes, after their meals.

저녁 dinner

A 토요일에 같이 저녁을 먹을래요?
Would you like to have dinner with me on Saturday?

B 미안해요. 토요일 저녁에 약속이 있어요.
I'm sorry. I have plans on Saturday evening.

A: 토요일에 _____ _____ _____?
B: 미안해요. 토요일 저녁에 약속이 있어요.

저녁 7시: 서울식당

QUIZ

2. Look at the picture and use "-(으)ㄹ래요" to complete the dialogue.

1)

영화를 보다

A: 유나 씨, 오늘 저녁에 같이 _____?
B: 네, 좋아요.

2)

한국어를 공부하다

A: 다니엘 씨, 오늘 같이 _____?
B: 미안해요. 오늘 피곤해서 그냥 집에 갈래요.

3)

놀다

A: 조나단 씨, 저녁에 우리 집에서 같이 _____?
B: 네, 좋아요.

4)

사진을 찍다

A: 우리 내일 공원에서 같이 사진을 _____?
B: 미안해요. 내일 좀 바빠요.

45 몇 시에 만날까요?
What Time Should We Meet?

 V-(으)ㄹ까요?

- **A** 우리 일요일에 만날까요? Do you want to meet up on Sunday?
- **B** 좋아요. Sure.

💡 V-(으)ㄹ까요?

This expression is used to ask the listener's opinion about doing something together. The subject of this kind of sentence is "우리."

받침 X	+ ㄹ까요?	만나다 → 만날까요?
받침 ㄹ		만들다 → 만들까요?
받침 O	+ 을까요?	먹다 → 먹을까요?

A 같이 점심 먹을까요? Do you want to have lunch with me?
B 네, 좋아요. OK, that sounds good.

✅QUIZ

1. Read the dialogue and conjugate the verb correctly.

1) A: 우리 산에 _____? (가다)
   B: 좋아요.

2) A: 같이 _____? (공부하다)
   B: 네, 좋아요.

3) A: 김밥을 _____? (먹다)
   B: 좋아요.

4) A: 우리 좀 _____? (쉬다)
   B: 좋아요.

5) A: 한국 노래를 _____? (듣다)
   B: 네, 좋아요.

6) A: 여기에 _____? (앉다)
   B: 좋아요.

A 같이 한국 음식을 만들까요? Want to cook some Korean food together?
B 네, 좋아요. OK, sounds good.

A: _____ 한국 음식을 _____?
B: 네, _____.

> **Culture**
>
> **이모티콘** Emoticons
>
> As more conversations take place through messaging applications, many people are using emoticons, which express emotions through a combination of letters, symbols, and numbers. When used effectively, emoticons can communicate emotions that words alone can't do justice to. In Korea, "^^" is a smile, "~" at the end of a phrase indicates a breezy tone, and "ㅠㅠ" shows someone crying. In English speaking countries, ":)" is a smiley face, ";(" is a sad face, and "XD" shows someone crying with laughter. One researcher has found a tendency for emoticons in Korea and other Asian countries to be read vertically and focus on the eyes and for Western emoticons to be read horizontally and focus on the mouth rather than on the eyes. People who don't use emoticons in their text messages can come across as more formal or less engaging. What kind of emoticons do you like to use?

2. Read the dialogue and conjugate the verb correctly.

1) A: 우리 같이 케이크를 _____ -(으)ㄹ까요? (만들다)

   B: 네, 좋아요.

2) A: 우리 공원에서 _____ -(으)ㄹ까요? (걷다)

   B: 좋아요.

A 무슨 한국 음식을 만들까요? What Korean food should we cook?
B 비빔밥이 어때요? How about bibimbap?

➕ **N이/가 어때요?** Asking for opinions

This expression is used when asking the other person's opinion about the subject of the sentence.

e.g. A: 무슨 선물을 살까요?
B: 꽃이 어때요?

✅UIZ

3. Read the question and write an appropriate answer using "-이/가 어때요?"

1) A: 어디에서 놀까요?
   B: _____? (노래방)

2) A: 뭘 먹을까요?
   B: _____? (피자)

3) A: 옷을 사러 어디에 갈까요?
   B: _____? (백화점)

46 토요일에 같이 저녁을 먹어요
Let's Have Dinner Together on Saturday

(우리 같이) V-아요/어요

A 토요일에 같이 저녁을 먹을까요?
Do you want to have dinner together on Saturday?

B 좋아요. 같이 저녁을 먹어요. Sure, let's do that.

토요일에 같이 저녁을 먹을까요? A

B 좋아요. ____ 저녁을 ____.

V-아요/어요 1

This grammar construction is combined with a verb to suggest something to the other person. (This kind of sentence is called propositive.) The verb ending here is the same as that used for informal declarative sentences (statements) and interrogative sentences (questions) in the present tense. When the verb's final vowel is "ㅏ, ㅗ," "-아요" is placed at the end. When the verb ends in "-하다," it changes to "-해요." When the verb's final vowel is not "ㅏ, ㅗ" and the verb doesn't end in "-하다," "-어요" is placed at the end.

ㅏ, ㅗ + -아요			-하다 → -해요		in all other cases + -어요		
만나다		→ 만나요	노래하다	→ 노래해요	먹다		→ 먹어요
살다	+ -아요	→ 살아요	운동하다	→ 운동해요	만들다	+ -어요	→ 만들어요
놀다		→ 놀아요	이야기하다	→ 이야기해요	걷다		→ 걸어요

살다 to live

A: 무슨 음식을 먹을까요? What kind of food should we have?
B: 우리 불고기 먹어요. Let's have bulgogi.

V-아요/어요 2

This grammar construction is mainly used when responding to questions that take the form "-(으)ㄹ까요?" The nominal subject of the sentence is "우리," but this can be omitted.

e.g. A: (우리) 뭘 먹을까요?
B: (우리) 불고기를 먹어요.

QUIZ

1. Complete the dialogue with the provided words.

1) A: 같이 청소할까요?
   B: 네, 좋아요. 같이 _____. (청소하다)

2) A: 어디에서 사진을 찍을까요?
   B: 우리 공원에서 사진을 _____. (찍다)

3) A: 같이 무슨 음식을 만들까요?
   B: 김밥을 _____. (만들다)

4) A: 우리 같이 좀 걸을까요?
   B: 네, 좋아요. 같이 _____. (걷다)

A 우리 몇 시에 만날까요? What time should we meet?
B 저녁 일곱 시에 만나요. Let's meet at 7 p.m.

➕ 몇 시에 어디에서? What time and where?

When making plans, it's necessary to talk about time and place. Here are two expressions to use when asking someone's opinion about when and where to meet: "몇 시에 어디에서 만날까요/볼까요?" "언제 어디에서 만날까요/볼까요?"

e.g. A: 몇 시에 어디에서 볼까요?
B: 오후 두 시에 서울식당 어때요?

Culture

우리 밥 한번 먹어요! Let's grab a meal sometime!

When characters are saying goodbye in Korean dramas, one character will often say something like "우리 밥 한번 먹어요!" (Let's grab a meal sometime) and the other will respond with "좋아요, 밥 한번 먹어요" (Sure, we should do that). But such remarks don't usually lead to concrete plans. For Koreans, a vague proposal for a shared meal is a conventional way of saying goodbye. In other words, it's a polite formula used to soften a goodbye with someone you don't know very well. So when someone makes a remark of this sort to you, it's generally better to assume they're just being polite than to try to nail down the details of when and where.

A 어디에서 만날까요? Where should we meet?
B 서울식당 어때요? How about Seoul Restaurant?
A 좋아요. 그러면 저녁 일곱 시에 서울식당에서 만나요.
   Sounds good. Then let's meet at Seoul Restaurant at 7 p.m.

A: _____ 만날까요?

B: 서울식당 어때요?

A: 좋아요. 그러면 저녁 일곱 시에 서울식당에서 _____.

QUIZ

2. Look at the picture and complete the dialogue.

1)

A: 언제 어디에서 만날까요?

B: 오후 다섯 시에 회사 앞에서 _____.

2)

A: 우리 같이 사진을 찍을까요?

B: 좋아요. _____.

3)

A: 같이 노래를 부를까요?

B: 좋아요. 같이 한국 노래를 _____.

4)

A: 같이 음악을 들을까요?

B: 좋아요. _____.

47 집에 가서 밥을 먹어요
I'm Going Home to Eat

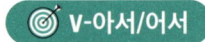

A 학생 식당에서 밥을 먹어요? Are you eating at the cafeteria?
B 아니요. 집에 가서 먹어요. No, I'm going home to eat.

V-아서/어서

- This grammar construction is used to indicate that following one action, another action occurs in connection with the first one.

"ㅏ, ㅗ" + -아서		
가다		→ 가서
오다	+ -아서	→ 와서
만나다		→ 만나서
일어나다		→ 일어나서

-하다 → -해서
요리하다 → 요리해서

in all other cases + -어서		
만들다	+ -어서	만들어서
쓰다		써서

- Some of the verbs that frequently come before "-아서/어서" are "가다," "오다," "만들다," "사다," "요리하다," and "일어나다."

  e.g. A: 아침에 일어나서 뭘 해요?   B: 아침에 일어나서 휴대폰을 봐요.

> ➕ **V-아서/어서 vs. V-고** Expressing connected vs. chronological actions
>
> - "-고" is used to express that two unrelated actions occurred in chronological order.
>
>   e.g. 미나 씨는 옷을 사고 친구를 만나요.

A 요리를 좋아해요? Do you like cooking?
B 네, 저는 보통 음식을 만들어서 먹어요. Yes, I usually make my own meals.

A: 요리를 좋아해요?
B: 네, 저는 보통 _____ _____ 먹어요.

Culture

혼밥 / 혼술 Eating and drinking alone

Eating out by yourself is known as "혼밥" in Korea ("혼" is short for "혼자"). Eating alone at a restaurant used to be a rare sight in Korea, and people who took up a whole table by themselves would sometimes get a bad look from the restaurant owner. There were even restaurants that refused to serve single diners, and restaurants specializing in dishes like 갈비, 삼겹살, and 부대찌개 would sometimes require a minimum order of at least two servings. But nowadays, more people are comfortable with the idea of eating out alone, and more restaurants are setting aside table space for such customers. So people dining alone have become more of a common sight. Another likely factor is COVID-19, which has made some people uncomfortable with the idea of eating in groups. Those circumstances have also led to the coining of the word "혼술," which means drinking alcohol (술) alone (혼자). Are 혼밥 and 혼술 things that you do frequently?

QUIZ

1. Combine two sentences into one using "-아서/어서."

1) 친구를 만나요. + 같이 운동해요.
   → _____

2) 저는 어제 백화점에 갔어요. + 옷을 샀어요.
   → _____

3) 저는 보통 아침에 일어나요. + 물을 한 잔 마셔요.
   → _____

보통 usually   일어나다 to wake up

A 친구 생일에 뭘 했어요? What did you do for your friend's birthday?
B 친구를 만나서 영화를 봤어요. I met my friend and watched a movie.

A: _____ 뭘 _____?
B: 친구를 _____ 영화를 _____.

➕ 입고 가요 Wearing something and going

When talking about "wearing" clothing somewhere, the required grammar construction is "-고."

e.g. 치마를 입다 + 가다 → 치마를 입고 가요. (O)
　　　　　　　　　　치마를 입어서 가요. (X)

　　 한복을 입다 + 오다 → 한복을 입고 와요. (O)
　　　　　　　　　　한복을 입어서 와요. (X)

➕ N을/를 타고 가요 vs. 걸어서 가요 Taking transportation vs. Going on foot

- When talking about taking a bus or train somewhere, the required grammar construction is "-고."

  e.g. 버스를 타다 + 가다 → 버스를 타고 가요.

- When talking about going somewhere on foot, the required grammar construction is "-아서/어서."

  e.g. 걷다 + 가다 → 걸어서 가요

한복 hanbok (traditional Korean attire)

A 친구한테 무슨 선물을 줬어요? What present did you give your friend?
B 모자를 사서 친구한테 줬어요. I bought a hat and gave it to my friend.

A _____ 무슨 선물을 _____ ?
B 모자를 _____ 친구한테 _____ .

QUIZ

2. Fill in the blank with the correct form of the verb.

1) 미나 씨는 불고기를 (만들어서 ☐ / 만들고 ☐) 먹었어요.

2) 수지 씨는 영화를 (봐서 ☐ / 보고 ☐) 저녁을 먹었어요.

3) 저는 한복을 (입어서 ☐ / 입고 ☐) 파티에 갔어요.

4) 어제 알리사 씨가 우리 집에 (와서 ☐ / 오고 ☐) 같이 놀았어요.

5) 친구 생일에 가방을 (사서 ☐ / 사고 ☐) 친구에게 줬어요.

6) 부산으로 버스를 (타서 ☐ / 타고 ☐) 여행을 갔어요.

7) 어제 친구하고 같이 맥주를 (마셔서 ☐ / 마시고 ☐) 치킨을 먹었어요.

48 다시 한번 말해 주세요
Please Say That One More Time

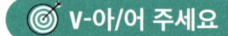 V-아/어 주세요

A 다니엘 씨, 창문을 좀 닫아 주세요. Daniel, can you please close the window?
B 네, 알겠어요. OK, I will.

 V-아/어 주세요

- This grammar construction is used in combination with a verb to ask for help or make a polite request. When the verb's final vowel is "ㅏ, ㅗ," place "-아 주세요" at the end. When the verb ends in "-하다," place "-해 주세요" at the end. And when the verb doesn't end in "ㅏ, ㅗ" or in "-하다," place "-어 주세요" at the end.

ㅏ, ㅗ + -아 주세요			-하다 → -해 주세요	
사다	+-아 주세요	→ 사 주세요	말하다	→ 말해 주세요
닫다		→ 닫아 주세요	전화하다	→ 전화해 주세요
오다		→ 와 주세요	이야기하다	→ 이야기해 주세요

in all other cases + -어 주세요		
기다리다	+-어 주세요	→ 기다려 주세요
만들다		→ 만들어 주세요
쓰다		→ 써 주세요

- You can make a request even more polite by adding "좀" before the verb.
  - e.g. 창문을 좀 닫아 주세요.

창문 window 닫다 to close 말하다 to speak 돕다 to help

A 수진 씨, 저를 좀 도와주세요. Can you please help me, Su-jin?
B 네, 잠깐만요. OK, just a moment.

➕ **도와주세요** Please help me

When the "ㅂ" batchim in "돕다" is followed by a verb ending that starts with "-아/어," the "ㅂ" turns into "오" rather than "우," resulting in the form "도와." Since "도와주다" (to help) is listed in the dictionary as a single word, the conjugated form "도와주세요" is also written without spaces.

e.g. 돕다 + -아 주세요 → 도와주세요.

QUIZ

1. Look at the picture and complete the sentence.

1)  죄송하지만, 사진을 좀 _____.

2)  저기요. 문을 좀 _____.

48 다시 한번 말해 주세요

A 수진 씨, 전화번호가 뭐예요? 좀 가르쳐 주세요.
What's your phone number, Su-jin? Can you please tell me?

B 제 전화번호는 공일공 일이삼사 구칠팔사예요.
My phone number is 010-1234-9784.

수진 씨, 전화번호가 뭐예요?
_____.
A

B
제 전화번호는
공일공 일이삼사 구칠팔사예요.

010-1234-9784

➕ **가르쳐 주세요** Please tell me

While "가르치다" often means "to teach," it can also mean giving someone information they didn't have before. So "가르쳐 주세요" can also be used in the sense of "알려 주세요" (please tell me).

e.g. 이름을 좀 가르쳐 주세요.

✓UIZ

2. Look at the picture and complete the dialogue.

1)

전화하다

A: 민수 씨, 지금 바빠요?
B: 네, 지금 좀 바빠요. 저녁에 다시 _____.

2)

오다

A: 토요일 저녁에 우리 집에서 파티를 할 거예요.
   일곱 시까지 _____.
B: 네, 알겠어요.

A 수진 씨, 미안해요. 천천히 다시 한번 말해 주세요.
　I'm sorry, Su-jin. Please say that one more time slowly.
B 공일공 일이삼사 구칠팔사예요. It's 010-1234-9784.
A 고마워요. Thank you.

QUIZ

3. Look at the picture and complete the dialogue.

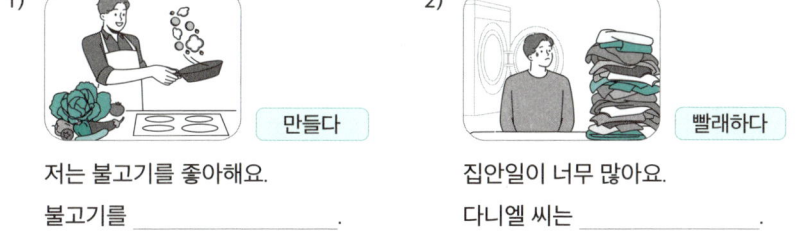

1) 만들다
저는 불고기를 좋아해요.
불고기를 _____.

2) 빨래하다
집안일이 너무 많아요.
다니엘 씨는 _____.

Culture

한국에는 팁 문화가 없어요 No tipping at Korean restaurants

At a full-service barbecue restaurant in Korea, servers will bring the charcoal to your table and grill the meat for you, too. You can even make simple requests such as "불판을 바꿔 주세요" (please change out the grill) or "고기를 좀 잘라 주세요" (please cut up the meat). But tipping isn't expected at Korean restaurants, so diners typically don't tip no matter how good the service was. If you would like to thank the waitstaff for great service at a Korean restaurant, it's really enough to say "감사합니다" (thank you) or "맛있게 잘 먹었습니다" (I really enjoyed the meal).

천천히 slowly　　다시 again　　집안일 housework

49 오늘은 좀 쉬고 싶어요
I Want to Rest a Little Today

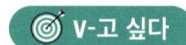 V-고 싶다

A 주말에 뭘 하고 싶어요? What do you want to do on the weekend?
B 부산으로 여행을 가고 싶어요. I want to travel to Busan.

 V-고 싶다

This grammar construction is used with a verb to express what the speaker wants to do or to ask the listener what they want to do.

	-고 싶다	
받침 ✗		사다 → 사고 싶다
받침 ○		먹다 → 먹고 싶다

부산 Busan

A 부산에서 뭘 하고 싶어요? What do you want to do in Busan?
B 생선을 먹고 싶어요. I want to eat fish.

QUIZ

1. Answer each question with an appropriate response.

1) A: 생일에 무슨 선물을 받고 싶어요?

    B: _____ .

2) A: 누구를 만나고 싶어요?

    B: _____ .

3) A: 저녁에 뭘 먹고 싶어요?

    B: _____ .

4) A: 주말에 뭘 하고 싶어요?

    B: _____ .

5) A: 지금 어디에 가고 싶어요?

    B: _____ .

6) A: 어디에서 살고 싶어요?

    B: _____ .

생선 fish (as food)   살다 to live

A 오늘은 좀 쉬고 싶어요. 우리 내일 만나요.
I want to rest a little today. Let's meet tomorrow.

B 알겠어요. OK.

➕ **알겠어요** OK

This expression is used to indicate that the speaker likes or approves of an idea or suggestion.

e.g. A: 주말에 산에 가고 싶어요.
B: 알겠어요. 같이 가요.

Culture

생선 vs. 물고기 Fish as food vs. Live fish

Foreigners sometimes say things like, "저는 어제 물고기를 먹었어요" (I ate fish yesterday). But is that the correct expression? The Korean word "물고기" refers to fish living in the rivers and ocean, or more precisely, living fish in the water. In contrast, "생선" refers to fish that are caught for eating. So the fish that are for sale at a market or store are "생선," not "물고기." So which is the one you eat—"생선" or "물고기"?

누구 who

A 누가 보고 싶어요? Who do you miss?
B 고향 친구가 보고 싶어요. I miss my friends back home.

➕ **N이/가 보고 싶다** Missing someone

This expression signifies that the subject misses somebody. Take careful note of the fact that "이/가" is placed after the person being missed.

e.g. A: 누가 보고 싶어요?
B: 동생이 보고 싶어요.

QUIZ

2. Match the sentences that go together.

1) 우리 내일 두 시에 만나요. •   • a) 엄마가 보고 싶어요.

2) 어디에 가고 싶어요? •   • b) 여기 있어요.

3) 누구한테 선물을 주고 싶어요? •   • c) 일본에 가고 싶어요.

                                                              • d) 알겠어요.

4) 누가 보고 싶어요? •   • e) 친구한테 주고 싶어요.

50 시험이 있어서 공부해야 돼요
There's a Test, So I Have to Study

 A/V-아야/어야 되다

A 주말에 뭐 할 거예요? What are you going to do this weekend?
B 주말에 집을 청소해야 돼요. I have to clean the house this weekend.

주말에 뭐 할 거예요? A

B 주말에 집을 _____ _____.

A/V-아야/어야 되다 1

This grammar construction (often translated as "have to" or "need to") is combined with a verb or adjective to express the obligation or necessity of some action. When the verb/adjective's final vowel is "ㅏ, ㅗ," "-아야 되다" is placed at the end. When the verb/adjective ends in "-하다," "-해야 되다" is placed at the end. And when the verb/adjective does not end in "ㅏ, ㅗ" or "-하다," "-어야 되다" is placed at the end.

ㅏ, ㅗ + -아야 되다			-하다 → -해야 되다	
사다	+ -아야 되다	→ 사야 되다	일하다	→ 일해야 되다
작다		→ 작아야 되다	공부하다	→ 공부해야 되다
보다		→ 봐야 되다	따뜻하다	→ 따뜻해야 되다
좋다		→ 좋아야 되다	이야기하다	→ 이야기해야 되다

in all other cases + -어야 되다		
먹다	+ -어야 되다	→ 먹어야 되다
기다리다		→ 기다려야 되다
쉬다		→ 쉬어야 되다
쓰다		→ 써야 되다

A 언제까지 보고서를 써야 돼요? When do we have to write this report by?
B 금요일까지 써야 돼요. We have to write it by Friday.

✓UIZ

1. Look at the picture and complete the sentence.

1)  머리가 너무 아파요. 그래서 약을 _____.

2)  오늘 친구 생일이에요. 그래서 친구에게 _____.

3)  내일 아침에 약속이 있어요. 그래서 일찍 _____.

4)  늦었어요. 그래서 택시를 _____.

보고서 report   늦다 to be late

A 내일 같이 공원에 소풍 갈래요?
  Would you like to go with me on a picnic to the park tomorrow?
B 좋아요. 뭘 준비해야 해요? Sure. What do I need to bring?

A 내일 같이 공원에 소풍 갈래요?

B 좋아요. 뭘 _____ ?

A/V-아야/어야 되다 2

The grammar construction "-아야/어야 하다" can be used instead of "-아야/어야 되다," but the latter is more common in colloquial language.

e.g. 시험이 있어서 공부해야 돼요. = 시험이 있어서 공부해야 해요.

Culture

대학수학능력시험 - 듣기 시험 때 비행기 운항이 금지돼요. No flights during the college entrance exam

Every November, Korean students who hope to enter university take the 대학수학능력시험 (College Scholastic Ability Test), often abbreviated as 수능 (Suneung), which assesses their ability to complete university coursework. Since students' university admission depends on their score on this test, the Korean government takes a number of steps to prevent mishaps. Big corporations and government offices push back the beginning of the workday, financial markets open late, and more buses and trains are put into service as well. Most interestingly, planes are forbidden from taking off or landing at any airport in Korea during the 35 minutes of the English listening section to keep students from getting distracted. So if you're planning to fly on the day of the big test, be sure to check whether a flight is actually available.

소풍 picnic

A 주말에 놀이공원에 갈래요?
Would you like to go to an amusement park this weekend

B 미안해요. 다음 주에 시험이 있어서 공부해야 돼요.
I'm sorry. There's a test next week, so I have to study.

A: 주말에 놀이공원에 갈래요?

B: 미안해요. 다음 주에 시험이 있어서 _____ ____.

QUIZ

2. Look at the picture and complete the dialogue using "-아야/어야 되다."

1)

오늘 선물을 사다

A: 내일 유나 씨 생일이에요. 생일 선물을 샀어요?
B: 아니요, 아직 안 샀어요. _____.

2)

아르바이트를 하러 가다

A: 오늘 오후에 시간이 있어요?
B: 미안해요. 저는 오후에 _____.

3)

한국 사람하고 많이 이야기하다

A: 한국어를 잘하고 싶어요. 어떻게 해야 돼요?
B: 그러면 _____.

놀이공원 amusement park   잘하다 to do well

50 Days of Korean

부록 Appendix
정답 Answer Key
어휘 색인 Vocabulary Index

정답 Answer Key

01 안녕하세요? Hello!

1. 1) 안녕? — b. Hi! (casual speech style)
   2) 안녕하세요? — a. Hello! (polite speech style)
2. 1) 안녕히 가세요. — a. Goodbye. (go in peace)
   2) 안녕히 계세요. — b. Goodbye. (stay in peace)
3. ☐ 안녕히 계세요.
   ☑ 안녕하세요?
   ☐ 안녕히 가세요.

02 다니엘 하임이에요 I'm Daniel Heim

1. 1) 조나단 — b. 예요.
   2) 박서우 — a. 이에요.
   3) 마리아 칼라스 — b. 예요.
   4) 이나영 — a. 이에요.
2. 안녕하세요? 김유나 <u>예요</u>. 만나서 <u>반가워요</u>.

03 저는 독일 사람이에요 I'm German

1. 1) 영국 — b. U.K.
   2) 독일 — a. Germany
2. 1) 저 — a. 은
   2) 기음 — b. 는
   3) 마이클 — a. 은
3. 1) 네 2) 아니요

04 저는 학생이 아니에요 I'm Not a Student

1. 1) 가수예요   2) 의사예요
   3) 선생님이에요
2. 1) 이 2) 가 3) 가 4) 이

3. 1) 영우 씨는 학생이에요? — b) 아니요, 회사원이 아니에요.
   2) 수진 씨는 회사원이에요? — c) 아니요, 회사원이에요.
   3) 유나 씨는 중국 사람이에요? — a) 아니요, 한국 사람이에요.

05 지금 공부해요 I'm Studying Right Now

1. 1) 옷을 사요   2) 일해요
2. 1) 공부해요   2) 쉬어요
   3) 가르쳐요   4) 먹어요

06 커피를 좋아해요 I Like Coffee

1. 1) 을 2) 를 3) 를 4) 을
2. 1) 먹어요   2) 해요
   3) 마셔요   4) 해요

07 고기를 안 먹어요 I Don't Eat Meat

1. 1) e.g. 비빔밥을 안 먹어요
   2) e.g. 녹차를 안 마셔요
2. 1) 김치를 안 먹어요   2) 운동 안 해요
   3) 커피를 안 마셔요   4) 일본어를 공부 안 해요
   5) 고기를 안 좋아해요

08 집에 가요 I'm Going Home

1. 1) 학교에 가요   2) 회사에 가요
   3) 집에 가요   4) 병원에 가요
2. 1) d 2) c 3) b 4) a

09 집에서 밥을 먹어요 I Eat Meals at Home

1. 1) 에서 2) 에 3) 에서 4) 에서

2. 1) 카페에 가요   2) 공원에서 만나요
   3) 집에서 공부해요

10 수업이 없어요 I Don't Have Class Today

1. 1) 이   2) 가   3) 이   4) 가
2. 1) 있어요   2) 있어요
   3) 없어요   4) 있어요

11 물냉면 주세요
I Would Like Some Mul-Naengmyeon

1. 보세요   읽으세요   쉬세요
   요리하세요   앉으세요
2. e.g. 커피 주세요.
   e.g. 메뉴 좀 주세요.

12 참치김밥 하나 주세요
I Would Like One Tuna Gimbap

1. 1) 하나   2) 둘
   3) 김밥 셋   4) 비빔밥 넷
2. 1) 물냉면   2) 둘 주세요 / 양파
   3) 하나 주세요 / 달걀

13 맥주 두 병하고 소주 한 병 주세요
Two Bottles of Beer and One Bottle of Soju, Please

1. 커피 세 잔 주세요.
   사과 다섯 개 주세요.
   냉면 두 그릇 주세요.
   맥주 네 병 주세요.
2. 1) 사과 네 개하고 물 한 잔
   2) 샌드위치 여덟 개하고 콜라 아홉 병

14 천 원이에요 It's 1,000 Won

1. 1) 칠백   2) 천오백
   3) 사만삼천팔백   4) 백이십구만
2. 1) 뭐 드릴까요? — a) 하나에 천 원이에요.
   2) 물냉면이 있어요? — b) 네, 있어요.
   3) 이거 얼마예요? — c) 사과 열 개 주세요.

15 양념치킨이 맛있어요
Yangnyeom Chicken Tastes Good

1. 1) 가 맛있어요   2) 가 따뜻해요
   3) 이 싸요
2. e.g. 커피가 맛있어요.
   e.g. 김밥이 좋아요.
   e.g. 비빔밥이 맛없어요.
   e.g. 주스가 시원해요.
   e.g. 사과가 싸요.
3. e.g. 치킨이 어때요? 치킨이 맛있어요.

16 저녁에 운동을 해요 I Exercise in the Evening

1. 1) 저는 아침에   2) 저는 저녁에
   3) 저는 밤에   4) 저는 점심에
2. 1) 에   2) 에   3) × / 에
   4) × / 에

17 몇 시에 일어나요? What Time Do You Get Up?

1. 1) 여덟 시 이십 분 2) 한 시 삼십 분 3) 세 시 사십 분 4) 열 시 오십 분

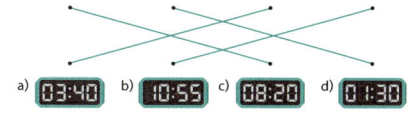

2. 1) ×   2) ×   3) ○

18 네 시부터 일곱 시까지 아르바이트를 해요
My Part-Time Work Goes from Four to Seven O'Clock

1. 1) 아침부터 밤까지
   2) 한 시부터 네 시까지
   3) 오후 두 시부터 오후 세 시까지
2. 1) 열 시부터 열두 시까지 한국어 수업이 있어요
   2) 한 시부터 세 시까지 한국어를 공부해요
   3) 여섯 시부터 열 시까지 아르바이트를 해요

19 무슨 요일에 아르바이트를 해요?
What Days of the Week Do You Work Part-Time?

1. 1) 일요일 — Sunday
   2) 화요일 — Thursday
   3) 금요일 — Wednesday
   4) 토요일 — Saturday
   5) 월요일 — Monday
   6) 수요일 — Friday
   7) 목요일 — Tuesday
2. 1) 월요일에 가요
   2) 화요일하고 일요일에 만나요
   3) 수요일하고 토요일에 해요
3. 1) 몇   2) 무슨   3) 몇
   4) 무슨   5) 몇
4. 1) e.g. 사과를 좋아해요
   2) e.g. 축구를 좋아해요
   3) e.g. 비빔밥을 좋아해요
   4) e.g. 월요일을 좋아해요

20 생일이 언제예요? When Is Your Birthday?

1. 1) 십이월 팔 일   2) 팔월 칠 일
   3) 오월 십 일   4) 유월 삼십 일
2. 1) 사월 십오 일이에요
   2) 사월 십칠 일이에요
   3) 사월 십구 일이에요

21 전화번호가 어떻게 돼요?
Can You Tell Me Your Phone Number?

1. 1) 열여섯 — a. 14살 / b. 16살
   2) 02-8975-6129 — a. 공이-육구사오-육이삼구 / b. 공이-팔구칠오-육일이구
2. 1) e.g. 저는 스물한 살이에요
   2) e.g. 공일공의 구팔칠육의 오사삼일이에요
3. 1) 연세가 어떻게 되세요? — c) 저는 쉰 살이에요.
   2) 성함이 어떻게 되세요? — a) 저는 히로 마사오예요.
   3) 직업이 어떻게 되세요? — d) 저는 선생님이에요.
   4) 전화번호가 어떻게 되세요? — b) 010-3789-49967이에요.

22 은행이 어디에 있어요? Where Is the Bank?

1. 1) 삼 층에 있어요   2) 이 층에 있어요
   3) 일 층에 있어요
2. 1) 옆에 있어요   2) 미용실이 있어요
   3) 아래에 있어요

23 아래층으로 가세요 Go Downstairs

1. 1) 으로   2) 로 / 로
   3) 으로   4) 로
2. 1) 로   2) 로
   3) 으로   4) 로
3. 1) 에   2) 에서
   3) 에   4) 으로
   5) 에 / 으로

24 어제 집에서 쉬었어요
I Rested at Home Yesterday

1. 1) 갔어요   2) 먹어요
   3) 해요   4) 만났어요
   5) 봤어요   6) 일어나요
2. 1) 먹었어요   2) 샤워했어요
   3) 만났어요   4) 갔어요

5) 봤어요   6) 마셨어요
7) 했어요   8) 재미있었어요

3) 금요일이나 토요일에 만나요

25 책을 읽고 잤어요
I Read a Book and Went to Bed

1. 1) 배우고   2) 하고
   3) 보고   4) 하고
2. 1) 가고   2) 하고
   3) 싸고   4) 하고
   5) 가르치고

26 순두부찌개가 맵지만 맛있어요
Sundubu-jjigae Is Spicy, but It Tastes Good

1. 1) 맛있지만 비싸요
   2) 어렵지만 재미있어요
   3) 싸지만 맛없어요
2. 1) 저는 김치를 좋아하지만 친구는 김치를 안 먹어요
   2) 어제는 도서관에 갔지만 오늘은 집에서 쉬어요
   3) 전에는 김치를 안 먹었지만 지금은 김치를 먹어요

27 유튜브를 보거나 책을 읽어요
I Watch YouTube or Read a Book

1. 1) 먹거나 / 마셔요
   2) 가거나 / 운동해요
   3) 사거나 / 만나요
2. e.g. 저는 주말에 공부하거나 친구를 만나요.

28 빨래나 청소를 해요
I Do the Laundry or the Cleaning

1. 1) 이나   2) 나   3) 나   4) 이나
2. 1) 수영이나 태권도를 해요
   2) 파스타나 샐러드나 피자를 만들어요

29 방학에 고향에 갈 거예요
I'm Going to Go to My Hometown for the Vacation

1. 1) 공부했어요.   2) 만날 거예요.
   3) 운동했어요.   4) 갈 거예요.
2. 1) 만날 거예요 /
      e.g. 네, 저는 내일 친구를 만날 거예요.
   2) 운동할 거예요 /
      e.g. 아니요, 내일 운동 안 할 거예요.
   3) 살 거예요 /
      e.g. 저는 내일 백화점에서 옷을 살 거예요.
   4) 먹을 거예요 /
      e.g. 저는 내일 비빔밥을 먹을 거예요.
   5) 만날 거예요 /
      e.g. 저는 내일 친구를 만날 거예요.

30 그냥 집에서 쉬려고 해요
I'm Just Planning to Relax at Home

1. 1) 하려고 해요   2) 만나려고 해요
   3) 청소하려고 해요 4) 찍으려고 해요
2. 1) 사려고 했어요   2) 하려고 했어요
   3) 가려고 했어요   4) 하려고 했어요

31 기차로 부산에 갈 거예요
I'm Going to Go to Busan by Train

1. 1) 로   2) 로   3) 로
   4) 로   5) 으로
2. e.g. 밥을 뭐로 먹어요?
       숟가락으로 먹어요.
   e.g. 떡볶이를 뭐로 먹어요?
       포크로 먹어요.

32 부산까지 얼마나 걸려요?
How Long Does It Take to Get to Busan?

1. 1) 에서 2) 까지
   3) 에서 / 까지 4) 에서 / 까지
2. 1) A: 회사에서 집까지 / B: 15분쯤 걸려요
   2) A: 호텔에서 공항까지 / B: 40분쯤 걸려요
   3) A: 서울에서 전주까지 / B: 두 시간쯤 걸려요

33 생일이 언제예요? I Go Home on Foot

1. 1) 걸어서 가요 / 5분쯤 걸려요
   2) 지하철로 갔어요 / 30분쯤 걸렸어요
2. 1) 들어요 2) 걷고
   3) 들었어요 4) 걸으려고 해요
   5) 듣거나

34 KTX가 아주 빨라요 The KTX Is Very Fast

1. 1) 빨라요 2) 몰라요
   3) 잘라요 4) 불러요
2. 1) 잘랐어요 2) 불렀어요
   3) 부를 거예요 4) 자를 거예요

35 머리가 아파요 My Head Hurts

1.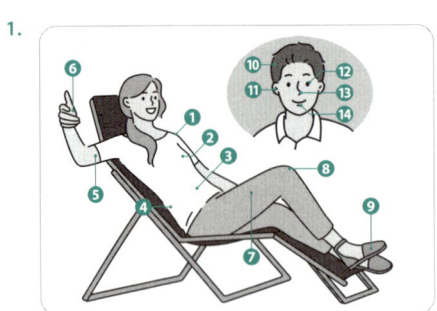

a. 어깨 [1] h. 허리 [4]
b. 팔 [5] i. 무릎 [8]
c. 배 [3] j. 코 [13]
d. 발 [9] k. 귀 [11]
e. 손 [6] l. 눈 [12]
f. 가슴 [2] m. 입 [14]
g. 다리 [7] n. 머리 [10]

2. 1) 배가 아파요 2) 어깨가 아파요
   3) 다리가 아파요
3. 1) 바빠요 2) 예뻐요
   3) 써요 4) 아팠어요

36 오늘 날씨가 추워요 The Weather Is Cold Today

1. 1) 매워요 2) 더워요
   3) 어려워요 4) 추워요
2. 2) 는 / 흐려요 3) 는 / 맑아요

37 어느 계절을 좋아해요?
Which Season Do You Like?

1. 1) 봄 — winter
   2) 여름 — fall
   3) 가을 — spring
   4) 겨울 — summer
2. 1) e.g. 겨울을 좋아해요
   2) e.g. 프랑스 사람이에요
   3) e.g. 한국 식당에서 자주 먹어요
3. 1) 무슨 2) 어느 3) 어느 4) 무슨
   5) 무슨 6) 어느

38 추워서 겨울을 안 좋아해요
I Don't Like Winter Because It's Cold

1. 1) 비싸서 안 사요
   2) 피곤해서 집에 일찍 가요
   3) 바빠서 친구를 안 만나요

2. 1) 너무 바빠서 안 갔어요
   2) 너무 아파서 안 갔어요
   3) 많이 먹어서 배불러요
   4) 많이 자서 안 피곤해요

39 눈이 많이 와서 산에 못 갔어요
It Snowed a Lot, So I Couldn't Go to the Mountain

1. 1) 못 만났어요 2) (운전) 못 해요
   3) 못 샀어요 4) (운동) 못 했어요
2. 1) 눈이 와요 2) 비가 와요
3. 1) 안 2) 못 3) 안
   4) 안 5) 안 6) 못

40 누구의 가방이에요? Whose Bag Is It?

1. 2) 조나단의 자전거예요
   3) 유나의 볼펜이에요
   4) 마리아의 구두예요
2. 1) 이거는 제 공책이에요
   2) 다니엘의 우산이에요
   3) 이거는 제 시계예요
   4) 마리의 휴대폰이에요

41 동생한테 선물을 보내려고 해요
I'm Planning to Send a Present to My Younger Sibling

1. 1) 에 2) 이 3) 에 4) 에서
   5) 을 6) 하고 7) 에 8) 한테
2. 1) 한테 2) 께 3) 한테
   4) 께 5) 에

42 친구한테서 꽃을 받았어요
I Got Flowers from a Friend

1. 1) 유나한테서 2) 친구한테서
   3) 고향 친구한테서

2. 1) 에 2) 에게 3) 에게서 4) 에서

43 옷을 사러 백화점에 갈 거예요
I'm Going to Go to the Department Store to Buy Clothes

1. 1) 책을 읽으러 2) 영화를 보러
   3) 일하러 4) 사과를 사러
2. 1) 사러 2) 타러
   3) 와서 4) 사러
   5) 걸어서 6) 놀러

44 같이 저녁을 먹을래요?
Would You Like to Have Dinner with Me?

1. 1) 쉴래요 2) 읽을래요
   3) 갈래요
2. 1) 영화를 볼래요? 2) 한국어를 공부할래요?
   3) 놀래요? 4) 찍을래요?

45 몇 시에 만날까요? What Time Should We Meet?

1. 1) 갈래요? 2) 공부할래요?
   3) 먹을래요? 4) 쉴래요?
   5) 들을래요? 6) 앉을래요?
2. 1) 만들까요? 2) 걸을까요?
3. 1) 노래방이 어때요? 2) 피자가 어때요?
   3) 백화점이 어때요?

46 토요일에 같이 저녁을 먹어요
Let's Have Dinner Together on Saturday

1. 1) 청소해요 2) 찍어요
   3) 만들어요 4) 걸어요
2. 1) 만나요 2) 같이 사진을 찍어요
   3) 불러요 4) 같이 음악을 들어요

47 집에 가서 밥을 먹어요 I'm Going Home to Eat

1. 1) 친구를 만나서 같이 운동해요
   2) 저는 어제 백화점에 가서 옷을 샀어요
   3) 저는 보통 아침에 일어나서 물을 한 잔 마셔요
2. 1) 만들어서   2) 보고
   3) 입고   4) 와서
   5) 사서   6) 타고
   7) 마시고

48 다시 한번 말해 주세요 Please Say That One More Time

1. 1) 찍어 주세요   2) 열어 주세요
2. 1) 전화해 주세요 2) 와 주세요
3. 1) 만들어 주세요 2) 빨래해 주세요

49 오늘은 좀 쉬고 싶어요 I Want to Rest a Little Today

1. 1) e.g. 지갑을 받고 싶어요
   2) e.g. 친구를 만나고 싶어요
   3) e.g. 불고기를 먹고 싶어요
   4) e.g. 등산을 가고 싶어요
   5) e.g. 공원에 가고 싶어요
   6) e.g. 부산에서 살고 싶어요
2. 1) 우리 내일 두 시에 만나요. — d) 알겠어요.
   2) 어디에 가고 싶어요? — c) 일본에 가고 싶어요.
   3) 누구한테 선물을 주고 싶어요? — e) 친구한테 주고 싶어요.
   4) 누가 보고 싶어요? — a) 엄마가 보고 싶어요.
   · b) 여기 있어요.

50 시험이 있어서 공부해야 돼요 There's a Test, So I Have to Study

1. 1) 먹어야 돼요   2) 전화해야 돼요
   3) 일어나야 돼요 4) 타야 돼요
2. 1) 오늘 선물을 사야 돼요
   2) 아르바이트를 하러 가야 돼요
   3) 한국 사람하고 많이 이야기해야 돼요

어휘 색인 Vocabulary Index

ㄱ

가다 to go	42	
가르치다 to teach	33	
가수 singer	26	
가슴 chest	150	
가을 fall	158	
개 general counting unit	62	
겨울 winter	158	
결혼식 wedding	174	
계절 season	158	
고기 meat	38	
고양이 cat	174	
고향 hometown	126	
공부하다 to study	31	
공원 park	44	
공책 notebook	173	
공항 airport	44	
과 unit (in a textbook)	82	
교실 classroom	104	
구두 dress shoes	171	
국 soup	137	
귀 ear	150	
그 that	114	
그냥 just, only	130	
그래요? Is that so?	24	
그럼 then, in that case	73	
그릇 bowl	62	
그저께 the day before yesterday	76	
금요일 Friday	86	
기다리다 to wait	33	
기자 reporter	26
기차 train	134
김밥 gimbap	35
김치 kimchi	35
꽃 flower	153
끝 end	82

ㄴ

나쁘다 to be bad	150
내일 tomorrow	76
냉면 naengmyeon	39
너무 too (much)	152
네 Yes	24
녹차 green tea	39
놀다 to hang out	184
놀이공원 amusement park	213
누구 who	208
눈 eye	150
눈 snow	167
눈이 오다 it snows	167
늦다 to be late	211

ㄷ

다르다 to be different	146
다리 leg	150
다시 again	205
닫다 to close	202
달걀 egg	61
달러 dollar	67
닭고기 chicken	38

덥다 to be hot	154		모자 hat	51
더 more	57		목 neck	150
독일 Germany	22		목요일 Thursday	86
독일 사람 German (person)	22		무릎 knee	150
돈 money	51		무슨 which, what	86
돕다 to help	154		물건 thing, item	120
동생 younger sibling	174		뭐 what	31
돼지고기 pork	38		미용실 hair salon	99
뒤 behind	100			
따뜻하다 to be warm	70		**ㅂ**	
떡볶이 tteokbokki	38		바쁘다 to be busy	150
			밖 outside	100
ㅁ			받다 to receive, get	178
마시다 to drink	33		발 foot	150
만나다 to meet	30		밤 night	74
만나서 반가워요. It's nice to meet you.	21		밥 rice, a meal	32
만들다 to make	126		방학 (school) vacation	126
많다 to be a lot	162		배 stomach	150
많이 many, a lot	109		배우 actor	26
말하다 to speak	202		배우다 to learn	32
맑다 to be clear	154		배터리 battery	133
맛없다 to taste bad	70		백화점 department store	44, 104
맛있다 to taste good	70		버스 bus	104
맥주 beer	35		병 bottle	62
맵다 to be spicy	114		병원 hospital	43
머리 hair	147		보고서 report	211
머리 head	150		보다 to see	30
먹다 to eat	32		보통 usually	74, 199
먼저 first, ahead	109		볼펜 ballpoint pen	51
멀다 to be far	115		봄 spring	158
며칠 what date	90		부르다 to call	146
모레 the day after tomorrow	76		분 the minute (when telling time)	78
모르다 to not know	146		불고기 bulgogi	39

비 rain	167
비가 오다 it rains	167
비빔밥 bibimbap	39
비싸다 to be expensive	73
빌리다 to borrow	178
빠르다 to be fast	146

ㅅ

사다 to buy	30
사람 person	22
사이 between	100
사진을 찍다 to take a photograph	131
살다 to live	194
샌드위치 sandwich	64
샐러드 salad	125
생선 fish	38
선물 present, gift	174
선생님 teacher	26
성함 name (honorific)	96
소고기 beef	38
소포 package	177
소풍 picnic	212
손 hand	137
수업 class	52
수요일 Wednesday	86
숙제 homework	52
숟가락 spoon	137
쉬다 to rest	32
쉰 fifty (pure Korean number)	97
쉽다 to be easy	154
스테이크 steak	137
스포츠센터 fitness center	184
시 the hour (when telling time)	78
시간 time	52
시간 time, hour	78
시원하다 to be cool, refreshing	155
시험을 잘 못 보다 to do poorly on a test	116
시험 test	52
식당 restaurant	43
싸다 to be cheap	70
쓰다 write	150
씨 Mr/Ms. (an honorific suffix used with names)	20

ㅇ

아니다 to not be (someone/something)	28
아니요 no	24
아래/밑 below	100
아르바이트 part-time job	84
아이스크림 ice cream	34
아주 very	35
아직 still, yet	133
아침 morning	74
아침(밥) breakfast	81
아프다 to hurt, to be sick	150
안 inside	100
안녕하세요? Hello (informal polite speech style)	14
안녕하십니까? Hello (formal polite speech style)	14
안녕히 가세요 Goodbye (go in peace)	16
안녕히 계세요 Goodbye (stay in peace)	16
안녕 Hi (casual speech style)	15
앞 in front of	100
야채김밥 veggie gimbap	61
약 medicine	168

약국 pharmacy	43	요즘 nowadays	117
약속 promise, appointment	52	우산 umbrella	50
양파 onion	61	우유 milk	39
어깨 shoulder	150	우체국 post office	174
어디 where	44	운동하다 to exercise	31
어떻게 how	94	원 won (the currency)	67
어렵다 to be difficult	115	월 month	90
어제 yesterday	76	월요일 Monday	86
언제 when	76	위 above	100
얼마 how much	67	유로 euro	67
얼마나 how long	140	은행 bank	98
없다 to not have	52	음식을 만들다 to make food	125
에이티엠 ATM	101	음악 music	142
여기 here	48	의사 doctor	26
여름 summer	158	이거 this	69
여행 trip	104	이다 to be (the base form of "이에요/예요")	18
연구원 researcher	26	인사하다 to greet	177
연세 age (honorific)	97	인터넷 internet	137
영국 United Kingdom(U.K.)	22	인터넷을 하다 to use the internet	124
영국 사람 English (person)	22	일 day	90
영화관 movie theater	44	일 work	52
옆 beside	100	일어나다 to wake up	81
예매하다 to book	137	일요일 Sunday	86
예쁘다 to be pretty	150	일찍 early	163
오늘 today	43	일하다 to work	31
오다 to come	30	읽다 to read	32
오른쪽 the right side	104	입 mouth	150
오전 a.m.	74	있다 to have, to be (somewhere)	50
오후 p.m.	74	이 this	82
왜 why	133		
왼쪽 the left side	104	ㅈ	
요리하다 to cook	36	자다 to sleep	30
요일 day of the week	86	자르다 to cut	146

자주 often	116		청소하다 to clean	36
잔 cup, glass	62		춥다 to be cold	154
잘 well	147		층 floor	98
잘하다 to do well	213		친구 friend	43
저기 over there	48			
저녁 evening	74		**ㅋ**	
저녁(밥) dinner	81		카드 (credit) card	136
전 in the past	117		카페 cafe	44
점심 lunch time	74		칼 knife	137
점심(밥) lunch	81		커피 coffee	33
젓가락 chopsticks	134		케이크 cake	137
좁다 to be narrow	154		콜라 cola	39
좋다 to be good	70		코 nose	150
좋아하다 to like	34			
주다 to give	32		**ㅌ**	
주말 weekend	86		태권도 taekwondo	168
주스 juice	39		토요일 Saturday	86
지금 (right) now	31			
지우개 eraser	51		**ㅍ**	
지하철 subway	134		파스타 pasta	125
직업 job	26		파티 party	90
집안일 housework	205		팔 arm	150
집 home, house	42		편의점 convenience store	44
쭉 straight (ahead)	105		포크 fork	137
쯤 around (a time or number)	81		표 ticket	136
			피곤하다 to be tired	133
ㅊ			피자 pizza	125
참치김밥 tuna gimbap	58			
창문 window	202		**ㅎ**	
차 car	50		하나에 per item	69
차 tea	35		하루 종일 all day long	165
처음 beginning	82		학교 school	43
천천히 slowly	205		학생 student	26

학생 식당 school cafeteria	115
한복 hanbok (traditional Korean attire)	200
햄버거 hamburger	64
허리 back	150
헤어스타일 hairstyle	149
호텔 hotel	138
화요일 Tuesday	86
화장실 restroom	102
회사원 office worker	26
회사 company	43
휴대폰 mobile phone	51
휴지 toilet paper	51
흐리다 to be cloudy	155